GHOST INVESTIGATOR

Volume 9
Back From the Dead

Written by
Linda Zimmermann

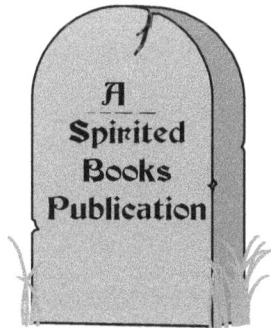

A Spirited Books Publication

Also by Linda Zimmermann

Bad Astronomy
Forging a Nation
Civil War Memories
Ghosts of Rockland County
Haunted Hudson Valley
More Haunted Hudson Valley
Haunted Hudson Valley III
A Funny Thing Happened on the Way to Gettysburg
Rockland County: Century of History
Mind Over Matter
Home Run
Ghost Investigator, Volume 1: Hauntings of the Hudson Valley
Ghost Investigator, Volume 2: From Gettysburg, PA to Lizzie Borden, AX
Ghost Investigator, Volume 3
Dead Center
Rockland County Scrapbook
Ghost Investigator, Volume 4: Ghosts of New York and New Jersey
Ghost Investigator, Volume 5: From Beyond the Grave
Ghost Investigator, Volume 6: Dark Shadows
Ghost Investigator, Volume 7: Psychic Impressions
Ghost Investigator, Volume 8: Back Into the Light

The author is always looking for new ghost stories. If you would like to share a haunting experience go to:

www.ghostinvestigator.com

Or write to:

Linda Zimmermann
P.O. Box 192
Blooming Grove, NY 10914

Or send email to: linda@gotozim.com

Ghost Investigator, Volume 9: Back From the Dead
Copyright © 2009 Linda Zimmermann

ISBN: 978-0-9799002-2-8

CONTENTS

Introduction

Last year as I was writing the introduction to Volume 8, I was facing some medical issues. I really don't want to get into it all, but suffice to say that I can now fully appreciate that there are worse things than death. Therefore, the title of this Volume 9, *Back From the Dead*, was derived not only from the subject matter of these cases, but my own personal ordeal.

Enough said, on with the introduction.

I was nothing short of astonished by several cases in this book… well, most of them, really. From the crashing sound and creepy photographs at the Patchett House, to the remarkable psychic validations at The Columns, Cliff Park, the train station, and the Greenfield Park Museum, these cases may just contain the strongest evidence to date of ghostly activity.

I could go on about the figure at the Tamarack, the child Mike encountered at Iron Island, or my return visit to Boulderberg Manor after eleven years, but I think I will keep this intro short and sweet and let you get straight to the cases.

So dim the lights, curl up by the fire, shut off your cell phone, and delve into my world—the bizarre, unsettling, but always fascinating world of a ghost investigator.

Linda Zimmermann
July 2009

Dedication

To all my family and friends who were there when I needed them.
Your love and support will always be cherished,
and will never be forgotten.

Patchett House
Montgomery, NY

I have certainly been surprised on investigations. In fact, it happens a lot, but seldom has a place been so surprisingly different over the course of two investigations. From a benign and relatively uneventful first visit, to literally a slam-bang, shocking second night several months later, the Patchett House in Montgomery, New York, presented a Tale of Two Investigations. If was the calmest of times, it was the most frightening of times, we had no photographic evidence, we captured some terrifying images…

The house was originally built around 1824 as an inn on the Newburgh-Cochecton Turnpike. Little is known about the early history of the place and its owners. However, there is documented history beginning in 1891 when Arthur Patchett converted the structure into a one-family house. Patchett was a partner with William Crabtree, and together they operated a woolen mill that was right down the street by the Wallkill River.

A Catholic priest claimed that after the Patchett family sold the property the building was used to house priests, but no records have been found to corroborate that assertion. What is clearly

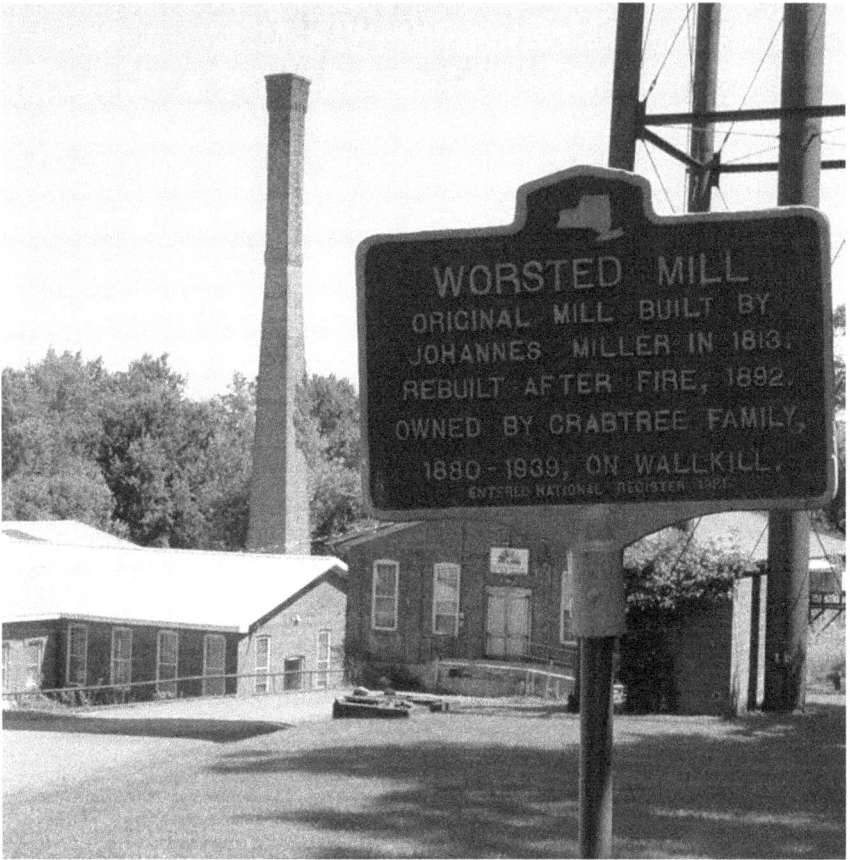

The mill that was once owned by Crabtree and Patchett.

documented, however, is the fact that the place became a funeral parlor. In fact, the three sinks where the bodies were placed for embalming still exist in the basement.

In 1977, the funeral parlor director ran off under suspicious circumstances, and the building remained vacant for twenty-five years. Those years of neglect took their toll, but fortunately one couple could still appreciate the beauty of place. They purchased the property and renovated the structure to house the Wallkill River School & Art Gallery. The WRS Director, Shawn Dell Joyce, also appreciates the beauty of the old inn and has devoted considerable time and effort to make it something of a sanctuary for local artists and students, where they can learn, teach, share ideas, and display

The embalming sinks in the basement.
(Infrared image.)

their work. On occasion, visitors can also have a rare glimpse into the past of the Patchett House, thanks to some unusual activity that paints this place directly onto the paranormal map.

So what type of things happen in this former inn/private home/funeral parlor? There is a phone that rings, which at first may not sound very unusual. However, when Shawn first heard the ringing there was only one phone installed in the house, and it had a modern electronic ring. What she heard was the sound of an old phone with a real bell, and she couldn't find the source anywhere in the building.

Others heard the phantom phone, as well. During a class she was teaching, the ringing phone echoed through the house.

"Aren't you going to answer that?" several people asked.

"I would if I could find the phone!" Shawn replied.

Several years ago, a member of the Patchett family was driving past the house. He pulled over to look at the place he remembered from his childhood, and there was his aunt Emma looking out her bedroom window at him. The only problem is that Emma had died many years earlier and the house was vacant!

Does the ghost of Emma Patchett stand by this second floor window?

Much of the activity here has been ascribed to Emma Patchett, and Shawn and others have felt a very helpful female presence on many occasions. However, Emma does have her little quirks, as it appears as though she does not like to have doors and windows left open. She won't make a fuss about it, she will simply close the door or window herself.

While some people have sensed a gentle female presence in the basement—which may or may not be Emma—there could be at least one other spirit down there that unnerves people. An electrician working in the basement felt a cold chill sweep through him. He screamed, dropped his tools, and ran out. He was so frightened by the episode he refused to return. Other people have also felt some unnatural energy pass through them in the basement. And one artist would not enter the former embalming room, as she insisted there was a woman standing in the doorway.

Then there are the lights that go on by themselves, objects that move, and myriad other signs that the Patchett House was never truly abandoned. With the long and varied history of the building and its paranormal activity, it all promised to make for a fascinating investigation. Or not, at least during the initial visit, but then there were mitigating circumstances.

When Mike and I arrived in October of 2008, a class was in progress at the Wallkill River School, so we couldn't set up our equipment right away. Shawn gave us an excellent tour of the house, highlighting where the unusual activity took place. We were also joined by reporter Matt Frey, who was writing an article on the place for a Hudson Valley newspaper.

Photo courtesy of Michael Worden.

Matt, Me, and Shawn in a gallery room.

As it was impossible to conduct an investigation while the class was in session, we discussed past cases and how we go about doing what we do. Mike made an excellent point about some of these shows on television that go to a location that has over a hundred years of ghostly activity, but if they don't find anything in a few hours they declare that the place is not haunted. Little did we realize how that concept of no "ghosts on demand" would apply to the Patchett House.

The class participants eventually all departed, and Shawn also had to leave, but Matt bravely stayed behind. The building does take on a much different character when it is quiet and dark—especially the basement, and specifically the room that contains the embalming sinks.

While sitting quietly in the old embalming room, we saw an eerily glowing light in the adjacent room which caught our attention. All hopes of any paranormal origins were dashed, however, when we traced it to an LED light deep inside the furnace, which seemed to be an odd place to put a light. Matt made a good point about it when he said, "What function would that serve, other than to freak us out?"

Indeed, seemingly innocuous lights, objects, and sounds that go unnoticed during the hustle and bustle of the day can certainly be startling, or at the least puzzling, during the silence of night—particularly so in room where dead bodies were drained of blood and infused with embalming fluids!

The only possible inexplicable occurrences that night came when we were seated in the wide hall area of the second floor. Mike was trying to stir things up by challenging the spirits to give us a sign, and we did feel a cool breeze—but then it was an old house on an October evening, so we couldn't get too excited. Shortly after, we heard creaking floorboards beneath us on the first floor, as if someone was walking. Again, being an old house this simply could have been one of the building's natural sounds. Finally, there was the briefest of EMF readings in the attic.

So all things considered, as exciting as it was to tour this beautiful and historic house, it didn't register very high on the paranormal scale. But as the article Matt subsequently wrote quoted Mike as saying, "This place has been here for over 150 years, and we've been here for two and a half hours. We'll have to come back."

I did return a few weeks later to give a lecture and take part in the public ghost tours. It was a great venue for a lecture, as I always enjoy speaking "on location" at a haunted site. Afterward, the groups of visitors explored the creepy basement, the two floors of living space, and the attic. As the expansive attic has only a narrow strip of boards on which to walk, everyone had to be very careful where they stepped. While trying to maneuver along the line of people with my EMF meter, I took an ill-advised step backward. I don't know who it was who reacted quickly and gave me a helping hand, but many thanks for preventing me from stepping through the second floor ceiling!

I found some very interesting EMF readings this time, which had been all but absent on our first visit. Two "hot spots" appeared to be by the second floor bedroom window where the Patchett family member saw his Aunt Emma, and along the front wall of the middle bedroom on that same floor. The readings were consistent and persistent, and did not appear to be emanating from the walls themselves—where electrical lines could reside—but rather from discreet areas away from the walls and floor. It was certainly something to note.

Even though these two visits didn't provide any remarkable evidence, there were enough tantalizing tidbits and credible stories to warrant a full investigation when the house was completely empty. That chance came in April of 2009, and it would Mike, me, and Barbara Bleitzhofer. I was hoping Barb's psychic talents would shed some light on the house's many mysteries, but I must admit I wasn't expecting much in the way of other evidence. Was I ever wrong…

We briefly met with Shawn, who had other commitments that night, and then we were left alone in the house to get to work. Immediately upon entering, Barbara got a pain in her temple, and kept hearing the name Frank. Overall, there seemed to be a different atmosphere to the place that night, more of a sense of being on the defensive, but the early tension was quickly broken by an episode in the basement.

During our usual initial walkthrough, Mike came upon something in the basement that terrified him —a spider in one of the embalming sinks. From his reaction, Barb and I figured that the spider must be at least the size of a small horse, but in reality it was just an average household arachnid. It's simply that Mike doesn't care for "anything with more than four legs or less than two."

I pointed out that while he was "screaming like a little girl" I was capturing it all on my digital recorder, but he didn't care and continued to claim it was "the size of a dollar bill." He was also certain that it must be a poisonous spider of foreign origin, ultimately declaring it to be a "Peruvian Death Spider."

I really got a laugh out of that, as it was a running joke from last year when Mike and I were eating at an Indian buffet. The food was particularly hot that day, with one dish containing little peppers that packed more Scoville units than weapons-grade pepper spray. Catching his breath after eating one, Mike dubbed them "Peruvian Death Peppers" for some reason, and now we had the foreign killer spider to go along with them.

However, despite the threatening title, the tranquil little spider never moved from his comfortable spot in the dreaded Peruvian Death Sink, and we carried on with the investigation.

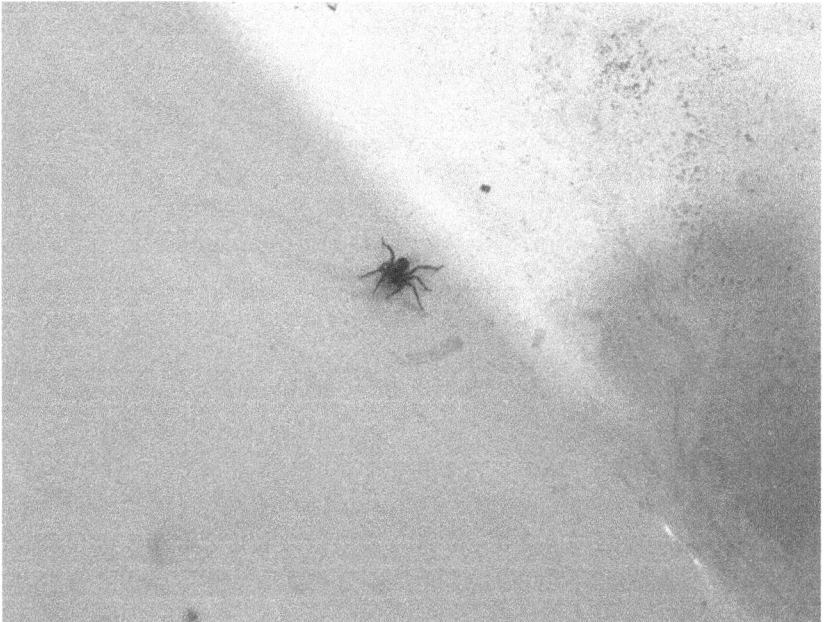

The fearsome Peruvian Death Spider.

Our plan was to set up Mike's new trail camera in the embalming room in the basement. It is one of those cameras that hunters use to get pictures of animals that happen to wander by and trip the motion sensor. He had been anxious to use it on an investigation, and was quite disappointed to find that the batteries had already gone dead. Fortunately, I happened to have bought some spare batteries that day so Mike was able to get the camera up and running. And given the nature of the images the camera captured that night, I shudder to think (or would that be shutter to think?) of how a few dead batteries almost prevented some of the most stunning photos we've ever seen from an investigation, but you'll just have to wait a few more pages for that. (Hey, no fair peeking!)

We moved back toward the staircase to another room where Mike decided to place a motion detector in the doorway. As he switched it on, he commented, "If that thing goes off and sounds an alarm we're leaving!"

Within minutes, a flurry of things happened in rapid succession—all culminating in the motion alarm going off!

We all felt a chill, and I kept picturing in my mind an unnaturally white man with his arms outstretched trying to come through that doorway, but he couldn't cross the threshold for some reason. I was beginning to think my imagination was running away with me, until Barbara said that she actually saw "something white moving in front of us." At that point the motion alarm started wailing. Believe me, it all made quite an impression on us, but we didn't leave.

We then heard some sounds coming from the room at the base of the stairs, so we slowly moved into that room. I was standing closest to the back wall, Mike was behind me, and Barbara was behind him, in basically a straight line. I was holding my K2 meter in front of me and was facing the wall. I was aware that two people were behind me, but I felt another presence as well, so I specifically said, "Is there someone behind me that can make the meter go up?"

Immediately I felt an icy cold sensation travel up my legs and throughout my body, and the K2 meter lit up!

"Yes, yes, yes!" I said in excitement. "Do you see it?"

"Oh my God! That is incredible!" Mike said in astonishment. "That's the most incredible EMF response I've ever seen. I'm blown away!"

And so was I. For those of you who may think I'm used to these kinds of things, let me assure you, I'm not. There we were in the basement of an old funeral home, we're already hearing and seeing things, and a motion detector was set off. Then I feel a strong presence behind me, which proceeds to sweep *through* my body with enough energy to light up my K2 meter like a Christmas tree. How could you ever prepare yourself or get used to something like that?

I thanked the presence for the quick and strong response, the meter stayed lit up for a few more moments, then returned to the single standby light. Just as I was taking a deep breath to relax a bit, Barbara took a sudden step backward and gasped. She had just seen the figure of a man descending the staircase. It was "black, husky, and shorter than Mike" and either didn't care that Barbara was able to see him, or wasn't aware that he was visible, as he didn't hesitate to come all the way down the stairs and walk right past her!

We waited a while longer to see what other evidence would present itself (a fancy way of saying what else there was that was going to freak us out). Fortunately for our nerves, it was quiet and uneventful—or so we thought—so we decided to head upstairs. Before leaving, however, Mike set up another motion detector. When I checked the audio the next day, I discovered that just after I asked him about the position of the detector, my digital recorder captured a long "Shhhhh!" which was much louder than our voices, and it wasn't anything we heard at the time. Perhaps someone was displeased that we were trying to track their movements?

We went to the second floor and chose the bedroom on the right front corner of the house (if you were looking at it from the street). We sat on the floor on different sides of the room with our cameras and meters. At one point, Barbara said the temperature had suddenly dropped several degrees, and both Mike's and my K2 meters lit up again. We tried to find a natural source for the strong EMF readings, but we could not find any logical explanation for them. And if it was faulty wiring or something natural, the readings should have been consistent, not coming and going, especially in response to our questions.

While in this bedroom, Mike—who was closest to the door—heard a noise from somewhere in the house and actually thought someone else had come in.

"Hello? Is anybody here?" he shouted down the stairs, but received no response.

Shortly after, my attention was drawn downward to the embalming room, which I realized, was directly below where I was sitting. I made a point of mentioning the time "in case something shows up on the trail camera." But as we were continuing to hear strange noises on the second floor where we were, my attention was drawn back to my immediate surroundings.

Mike took this infrared photo of me on the second floor as my attention is being drawn to the embalming room in the basement. Note that my K2 meter is lit up, indicating the presence of an energy field.

In order to try to place the origin of the sounds, we moved into the hallway near the banister. There is a mirror on the landing that gave a view underneath us of the front door, and Barbara saw a shadowy shape pass in front of that door. The figure had moved towards the dining room, but she "heard" that it wasn't the dining room, "it was the viewing room." Perhaps that room had been used to view the bodies when the place was a funeral home?

We didn't have time to ponder the former floor plan of place, because a minute or so later there was one of the loudest sounds I ever heard on an investigation—probably *the* loudest. It was like someone on the first floor picked up a piece of furniture and threw it across the room. I admit it startled me so badly that I gasped. Despite my fear, however, I started down the stairs.

"Let me go first," Mike said calmly, his hand on his gun. The noise was so loud he assumed someone had broken in, and he instantly switched from ghost detective mode to police detective mode. This was no longer the guy frightened by a spider, this was the seasoned cop on the job and prepared to defend us.

Barbara and I cautiously followed him to the first floor. While he checked the back door, I went to the front door—both were locked up tight. We slowly moved from room to room, but found no open or broken windows, and not a single thing was out of place. How could that be? Something big had just crashed to the floor, yet nothing was turned over, nothing had fallen from a shelf, and no pictures had dropped to the floor.

Fortunately, my trusty digital recorder had been on the entire time, and the banging sound came through loud and clear, so it wasn't mass hysteria or a group hallucination. What was equally shocking on the recording was what sounded like a deep breath or sigh just before the crashing sound. It just got creepier and creepier!

Since we couldn't find anything out of place upstairs, Barbara wondered if something could have knocked over Mike's trail camera in the basement. Of course we would have to check, but at times like this with things crashing around you in the darkness of an old funeral home, the last thing you really want to do is go into the basement where so much had already happened. However, concern for the safety of equipment trumps any fear!

Mike decided to turn on the basement lights before we went down there, and we had no objections. We carefully scanned each room to see if something had fallen, but found nothing. When we got back to the embalming room, we found that the camera was still on the tripod, apparently untouched...or so we thought at the time. When Mike checked the photos two days later, he found that something had touched the camera and made it move, and left some of the most frightening images we've ever captured.

First, let me explain how this camera works. When you turn it on, a motion detector is activated. When something moves in front of the camera, it triggers the shutter which then takes nine photos about three seconds apart. In daylight, the camera takes full color photos. In the dark, it takes infrared pictures. When Mike turned on the lights and we went to check on the camera, our movement set it off and it took nine color pictures of us and the room. However, sometime before that, Mike found that the camera had taken nine infrared photos in the dark while we were somewhere upstairs.

The day Mike saw these images, he immediately called Barbara and I. We were on the Garden State Parkway at the time, headed for Cape May (for some ghost investigating, of course), but after hearing the excitement in his voice I was tempted to turn the car around and go back to see these photos. But as our hotel was *supposed* to have wireless service, I asked Mike to email the photos to me and I would look at them on my laptop as soon as we checked in. Unfortunately, as it was early in the season and the hotel had just opened that week, they hadn't worked the bugs out of their wireless service yet, and I was unable to get a connection. It was very frustrating, but as the hotel was across the street from the beach and we were in beautiful Cape May, getting personal tours of haunted places, I couldn't get too upset!

When I got back home from the trip (which was a blast, by the way) I walked in the door, dropped my suitcase, and went straight for the computer. Mike had said that *something* was on the photos, but not exactly what it was, as he didn't want to influence my opinion. I don't quite recall what I was thinking I would find, but I guarantee it wasn't that large dark object directly in front of the lens! I just couldn't believe what I was seeing, and I also had no idea what I was looking at, but it certainly sent chills up my spine.

I immediately called Mike and we tried to figure out what it was. Several times we went over the timeline of the investigation, and were absolutely positive that after Mike set up the camera, we did not return to the basement in the darkness—only after Mike had turned the lights on did we go back down there, at which time the camera took the nine color photos of us.

Even though I had no doubt that none of us were in the embalming room when those infrared photos were taken, I suggested to Mike that he conduct an experiment to see what his hand would look like if he put it directly in front of the lens. While the overall shape had some similarities, the reflection off his fingers, the sharpness of the image, etc., all confirmed that it had not been a human hand in those photos.

Stealth Cam 04/15/2009 21:14:18 ● 55F

Something tripped the sensor of the trail camera, but
nothing unusual appears in this infrared photo of the basement.

As we were unaware at the time of what images had been captured by the trail camera, when we found that it had not been knocked over we simply returned to the investigation. We sat at the table in the room in the left front corner of the house, which is the room used for classes for the art school.

The pain in Barbara's temple that she first experienced when we arrived now suddenly returned. The temperature also dropped from 62 to 50 in a matter of minutes. Mike seemed to be particularly affected by whatever was happening and I asked if he was okay, as

Stealth Cam   04/15/2009   21:14:21   ● 55F

Three seconds later this dark object appears right in front of the lens.

In another three seconds, the object must be shaking
the camera as the background image is a complete blur.

Stealth Cam   04/15/2009   21:14:24   ● 55F

15

he was just not looking right. He couldn't exactly put a finger on it at the time, but someone appeared to be focusing their attention on him, and it was a heavy, depressing feeling.

We all were experiencing different things as we sat in the darkness, and my primary experience was that I began to smell something. At first it was faint and I couldn't determine what it was, but then it grew stronger and I knew right away.

"Gunpowder!" I suddenly blurted out. "It smells like burnt gunpowder."

Now, before any of you skeptical people out there ask how on earth I would know what burnt gunpowder smells like, let me tell you that I've fired off more than a few rounds in my day. I really loved skeet and trap shooting, and I used to also have a membership for an indoor target shooting range. I can say from experience that the smell of a spent shotgun shell is one of my favorite scents in the world. In fact, I've often said that they should make a men's cologne called "Spent Shell." But I digress…

Anyway, I couldn't imagine anything in the house that would cause such a smell, or why only now it was in the air. Mike agreed there was a distinctive gunpowder smell, and as I always say that the type of haunted activity reflects the message that the spirits are trying to get across, I thought perhaps I could put together some pieces of this paranormal puzzle. Barbara felt a sharp pain in her head, Mike was feeling distressed and depressed, and I was smelling gunpowder.

"Suicide?" I wondered out loud.

I asked some questions regarding a death in this manner, and when I asked if this spirit had been shot somewhere else and his body was brought here when it was a funeral parlor, Mike spoke up.

"I just had a horrible thought," he said with some hesitation. "Maybe he died on the embalming table."

A chill went through all of us when we considered the possibilities. Perhaps someone had attempted suicide or was shot in some other manner, was pronounced dead, but was actually in a very deep coma. Even with modern medicine people still wake up in the morgue, so it is feasible that someone had been brought to this funeral home and did not really die until his blood was drained— which would make for one very white corpse, wouldn't it? Perhaps the figure I envisioned and the white shape Barbara saw in the basement were additional clues to this man's fate? Of course, it's all speculation, but within the realm of possibilities.

Back to the facts we do know for certain—strange things continued to happen throughout the night. As we sat in the rooms on the right side of the first floor there were more unusual sounds throughout the house, and once again, my attention was pulled downward to the embalming room. When I glanced out the window from where I sat, I saw the metal cellar doors (now sealed) where the bodies used to be brought in, and realized that once again I was sitting directly over the embalming area. Mental note to self— choose another place to sit next time!

The cellar doors through which the bodies were brought in.
(Infrared image.)

As interesting and active as things were, however, we did not have a repeat of the "big bang" we had heard earlier, and we were disappointed that such an obvious sign escaped our direct experience. In other words, as crazy as it sounds, we had hoped it would happen again right in front of us. Since we were on the second floor when it occurred, I suggested that I go back upstairs, but have Barbara and Mike remain on the first floor in different rooms in case something happened again and we could try to triangulate the location.

So, as I climbed the stairs, Barbara sat in the back right room on the first floor and Mike was in the front right room. I reached the approximate spot where I had been standing the first time, made sure there weren't any squeaky floorboards, and then stood completely still and quiet, holding out my digital recorder. Only 20 seconds later I heard a grinding and banging sound below me, as if someone was dragging a metal chair. I assumed Mike or Barb had a folding chair and was adjusted its position, but thought I had better check to be sure.

"Was that one of you?"

"No!" Mike replied.

"What *was* that?" I asked again.

"That wasn't you?" Barbara asked.

"NO!" I replied emphatically.

Without any of us moving, we compared notes and agreed the sound had come from the first floor, somewhere in the main hall under where I was standing—just like the first time. Mike thought it had been me moving my chair, and Barbara also said she thought for sure it I had moved a metal chair, until I informed them I was standing perfectly still, and I didn't have a chair! In fact, as I looked around, I could see that there weren't even any chairs up there. As they could see each other at the time of the noise, they were able to confirm that they had both been seated and weren't moving either, so whatever it was hadn't been caused by any of us.

Fortunately, Barb and I both played back our audio recorders and we heard the grinding/banging sound. As remarkable as it was to capture such a noise, however, we heard something even more chilling. Ten seconds before that sound, both of our recorders once again captured what sounded like a deep breath! It was like whoever had caused the loud sounds wanted us to be certain it was not something natural, and that he had been responsible for both energetic outbursts.

The question now was, if an experiment worked twice, would it work a third time with Mike going upstairs alone? Perhaps it would have worked again, had Mike stayed upstairs long enough to find out! No sooner had Barb and I settled in the front and back rooms on the first floor, when Mike came right back downstairs. He said that as he reached the second floor landing he heard movement up there and it felt like hitting a wall of "horrible feelings." It was just too much after all we had experienced that night.

I asked Barbara if she wanted to try going upstairs alone, and she gave me a look and simply said, "Uhn, uh," the translation of which I believe is something like, "Are you crazy? No way!" As she had just felt someone touch her hair a few minutes earlier, I couldn't blame her!

We all agreed that we were sufficiently fried and had enough of the Patchett House for one night. Even without yet knowing what bizarre images were on Mike's trail camera, the banging and dragging sounds, the things Barbara was seeing, and the strong EMF readings in response to our questions, were more than sufficient to put this investigation near the top of the list for documented evidence. It was definitely a side of the Patchett House we had never seen before, and one that we weren't so sure we would want to experience again any time soon! Of course, given what happened after we left, we may not have to worry about ever conducting another investigation there...

I emailed the audio clips of the loud sounds to Shawn, along with Mike's trail camera images. I also wanted to thank her for giving us the opportunity to investigate the place. Her response shocked me. Apparently, all hell had basically broken loose the following day, and I felt terrible at the thought that we had somehow stirred things up, even though at no point were we ever antagonistic to the spirits.

Shawn had spent the next day alone in the Patchett House, and admitted it felt as though something had changed and there was an eerie feel to the place that hadn't been there before. She saw a dark shadow moving through the house, things kept "inexplicably falling to the floor," and a pipe burst in the basement, getting water all over her teaching materials. Was something punishing her for allowing us into the house? Were certain forces unhappy with us meddling into their affairs, and getting too close to the truth? It definitely seemed that way!

So, what can we conclude from our experiences and those of numerous eyewitnesses? The Patchett House is indeed haunted, at the very least by the kindly spirit of Emma Patchett, and perhaps other family members, or former guests/residents of the old inn. But there also appears to be a darker side, perhaps some less than happy spirits from the time that the building was a funeral home. While not threatening, these entities appear to want to maintain their anonymity. In other words, leave them alone, and they will leave you alone, which certainly seems to be the wisest course of action given the unpleasant repercussions.

Would I ever go back for another investigation? In a New York ghost investigator's minute! But I have to admit that for now, it may be best not to trespass into the world of the Patchett House's many restless spirits. There are enough problems in the world of the living without asking for more trouble…

Just how many spirits walk the halls of the Patchett House?

The Columns

I love history, and I'm particularly fascinated by the Civil War. I have vivid recollections of my visit to Ford's Theater in Washington, D.C., where I stood on the spot where John Wilkes Booth fired the fatal shot into the back of President Lincoln's head. I recall thinking of how different the country would have been if one of the wisest of American presidents had been alive to help guide the post-war years.

Ford's Theater also has an impressive museum of assassination and conspirator artifacts, and I thought I had seen just about everything there was to see regarding the event. However, there was one very important item of which I was unaware until recently, and relatively speaking, it's in my own backyard.

The Pike County Historical Society in Milford, Pennsylvania operates a museum in a beautiful, white mansion called The Columns, and their Civil War collection contains a unique piece of history—an American flag stained with the blood of Abraham Lincoln. As Lincoln lay mortally wounded in his theater box, part-time stage manager and actor, Thomas Gourlay, grabbed the large flag that was draped over the railing and placed it under Lincoln's head.

Gourlay kept that flag and passed it on to his daughter, Jeannie Gourlay Struthers, an actress who was in the play, *Our American Cousin*, which was being performed in the theater that fateful night. She later moved to Milford, and passed that precious piece of history on to her son, V. Paul Struthers, who donated the flag to the Pike County Historical Society in 1954. It is arguably one of the most historically important flags in American history, and the sight of the large blood stains can't help but send chills up your spine.

But that's not that only source of spine-chilling sensations at The Columns, as it also appears to be haunted. While no one claims to have seen Lincoln's spirit, the residual energy from the assassination flag could be adding to the intense paranormal mix from all the other items in the house. There's much more than meets the eye here, and it all led to one very remarkable ghost investigation.

The house was built in 1904 by

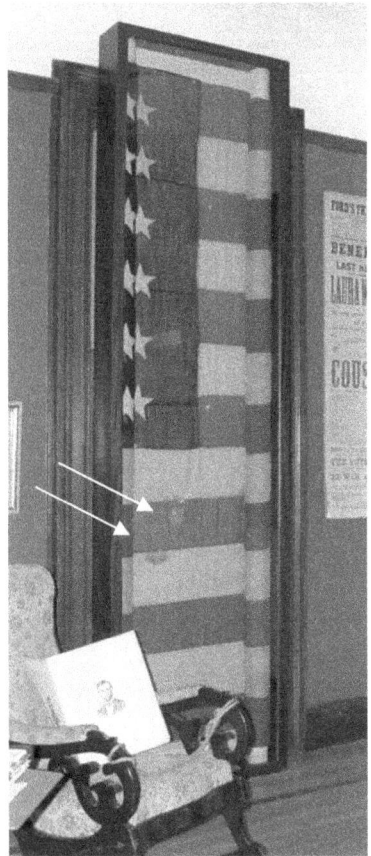

The arrows point to Lincoln's blood stains.

Dennis McLaughlin, an Irish immigrant who grew up in Jersey City, New Jersey, and made his fortune in real estate. According to information on the Pike County Historical Society web site:

"McLaughlin had four sons from his first marriage to Johanna Biggan, who passed away, and four children from a second marriage to Theresa Stack, who also died before McLaughlin. Strangely, both wives died on the same date of March 14th, 20 years apart. In the spring of 1912 Mr. McLaughlin took ill with what was described in the local newspaper, the Dispatch, as 'an attack of acute indigestion.' He was in residence at The Columns when the attack occurred, and promptly returned home to Jersey City where, a few days later, he died."

McLaughlin's children sold the house in the 1930s, and in addition to again being a private residence at times, it also saw duty as a boarding house, dance studio, VFW hall, night club, and restaurant. It wasn't until the 1980s that the Pike County Historical Society acquired the property and converted it into a museum.

Perched on a slight rise, this stately house with its six massive columns is definitely one of the most impressive structures in town. In the early 1900s, first-time visitors climbing the stairs from the road must have felt that they were about to enter someplace very special. Today, it remains a very special place, in some rather unique ways…

It was still light when Mike and I arrived one evening in May of 2009, and we took the time to admire the exterior and take plenty of photographs. What must it be like to have a place this extraordinary as your summer home? How many servants would there be at your beck and call to attend to everything from tedious little chores to preparing lavish parties? We both agreed that it must have been nice, and this was about as close as we would ever get to that kind of lifestyle!

We parked by the old Hiawatha stagecoach that had been wonderfully restored. However, no matter how good the condition is, I can't imagine bouncing along in that thing over hot, dusty roads, or on an icy, winter's day. I'm all for conservation and going green, but give me the automobile and its carbon emissions any day over a teeth-rattling stagecoach.

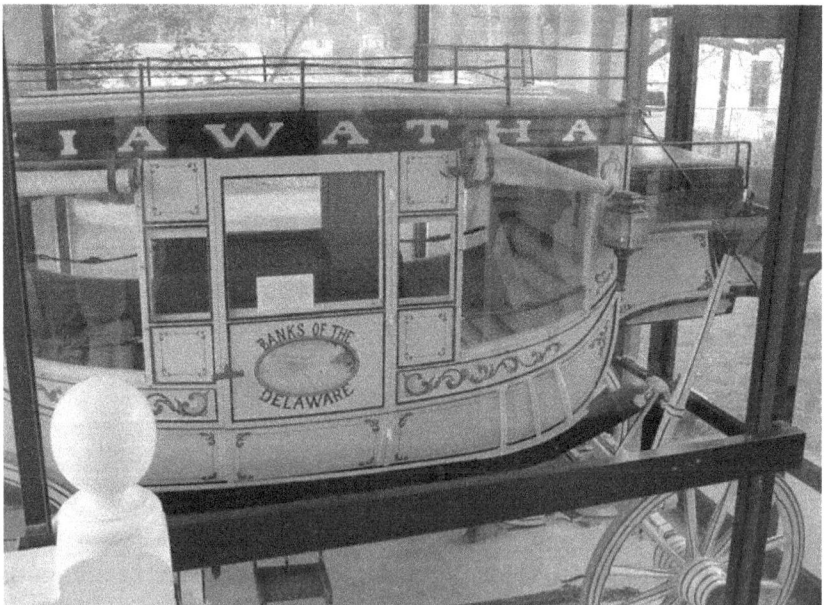

Mike unlocked the door and we started bringing in our bags of gear. I have to say that I hadn't taken more than a few steps before I felt extremely strong sensations—not quite a paranormal cream pie in the face, but a similar impact and sense of surprise. At the time I laughed and said something to the effect that this was going to be a very interesting night, but a short time later I wasn't laughing anymore.

We used the large foyer for all the equipment bags and before we could even unpack I had the very clear picture of an older woman standing by the banister on the second floor looking down at us. Her hair was swept up and her floral dress had puffy sleeves, a sash just below the bust line, and the skirt went straight to the floor (as opposed to a voluminous hoop skirt). I have to say that the scientific part of me was trying to block her out to some degree so I could concentrate on the meters and cameras, but she was not one to be blocked. My intuitive side was also saying to just accept whatever I was sensing now, and try to gather evidence to back it up later.

There were two other things that kept popping into my head—the name Beatrice, and something to do with opera. I had no idea what connection these things had to do with this place, but I got the sneaking suspicion that they might be ways of validating my impressions of the woman with the upswept hair. Perhaps it would be her way of saying, "I'm still here and you know it!"

While it was still light, we decided to take a quick walkthrough and see just how many rooms there were to cover. Of course, my first stop was the Lincoln flag. It was a solemn and humbling experience to stand before that flag and see the two darkened stains of blood where the dying president's head rested. What an incredible moment in history is represented in that flag—a terrible turning point that would have untold consequences for years to come, not to mention the loss of one of the most fascinating characters of all time. Lincoln loved Shakespeare, and Shakespeare would have loved creating a complex Lincolnesque leading man!

I had to resist the impulse to carefully examine every artifact in the Civil War room, as there were a few thousand square feet of mansion to cover. We quickly found that the place was even more enormous than we thought, and the rooms and staircases formed

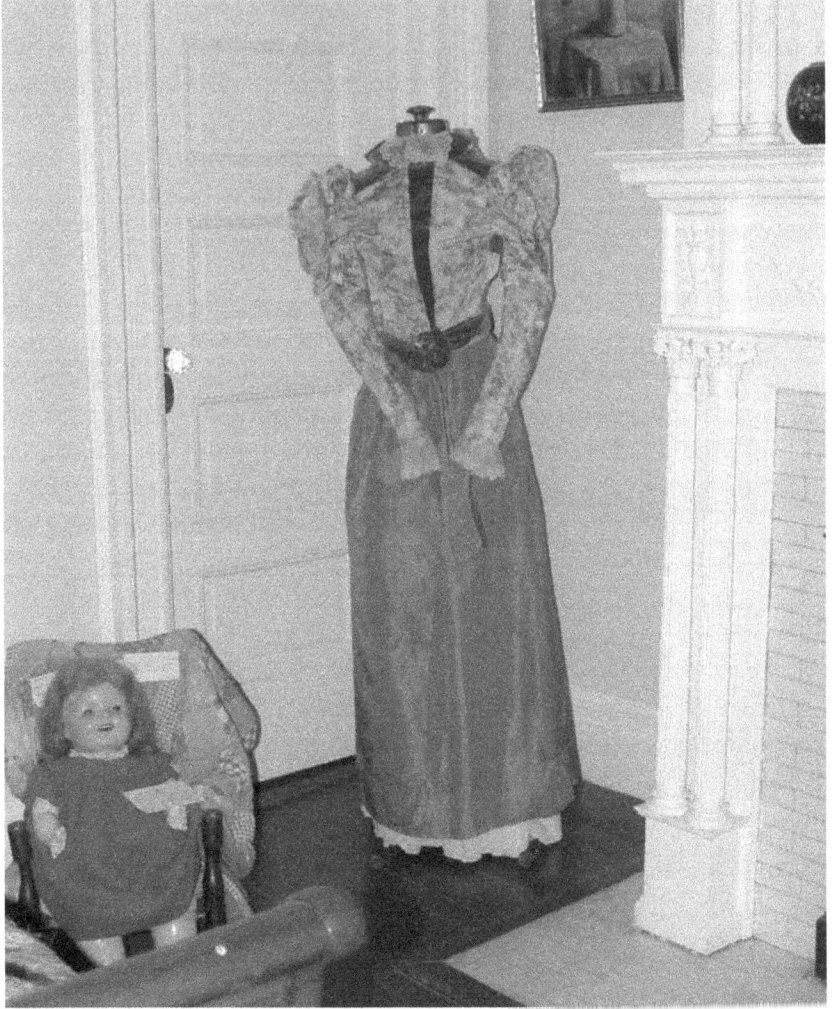

A dress on display on the second floor, which is the style I pictured the woman by the banister wearing.

something of a maze at first glance. I was regretting not bringing a bag of breadcrumbs so we could find our way back.

The main floor contained the Civil War room, a beautiful parlor with a curved seating area, offices, a library, several beautiful fireplaces, and incredible woodwork everywhere. There was a narrow and unadorned servant's staircase that led to the basement. One never knows what to expect in an old house, but this basement had a kitchen and a large finished lecture room, both of which minimized that old basement creepiness.

The second floor could be reached by the servant's stairs, or by the magnificent main staircase with its mahogany and stained glass—not to mention the spirit of the woman hanging out by the banister. I did feel a bit of a chill as we walked past that area, but there was too much yet to see to concentrate on that spot right away. There would be plenty of time later—she would make sure of that.

I was glad we knew about the taxidermy room, otherwise the sight of the stuffed wolf and bear may have evoked a more unpleasant reaction. A group of ghost hunters claimed that their batteries kept draining in this room, but we did not encounter any problems here that night. The second floor also contained bedrooms, a private study, and period dresses that appeared similar to the one in which I pictured the woman. After a quick tour of all the rooms on the second floor, we proceeded up another plain staircase to the third floor. Apart from the large skylight, there was nothing fancy about the small rooms on this floor, which had been servants' quarters.

On display: 20th Century Bear, 21st Century Ghost Investigator

This stuffed wolf is still on the prowl in the darkness of the museum. (Infrared photo.)

Both Mike and I felt uneasy right away on this floor, as if someone was not happy that we were there. Perhaps some former servant did not like anyone poking around in his/her private affairs? The uneasy feeling was not helped by all the manikins, and worse, pieces of manikins, we found in just about every room. It was a good thing we did not come upon our first decapitated head or grotesquely posed limb in the dark!

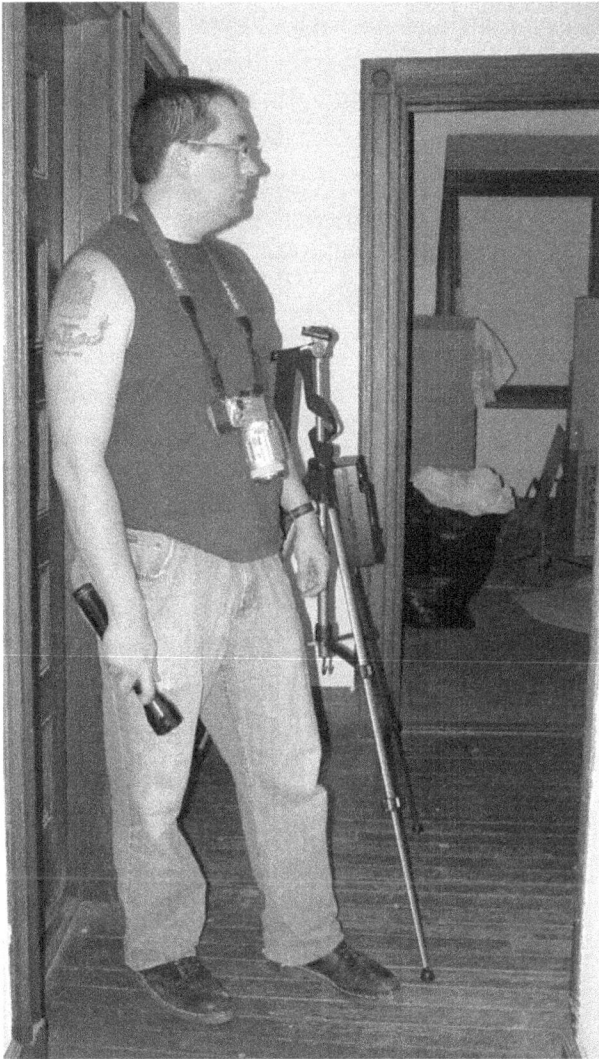

Mike is feeling uneasy and is "on alert" as he sets up the motion-triggered trail camera on the third floor.

There was also an attic, but with only a small floor area, we didn't think we would be exploring it in any depth—lest we take a wrong step and unceremoniously end up back on the third floor in a hurry.

Once our brisk, 10-minute tour of The Columns was complete, we returned to the foyer and laid out our game plan. But speaking of games, first things first—I turned on my radio to see how the Mets were doing. For a change they had a sizable lead so I was able to relax and concentrate on the investigation.

One of the first unusual things we experienced was a pounding sound, like a single "THUD" of a door being slammed or a heavy object being dropped. It was a low, deep sound that seemed to reverberate throughout the house. We tested floorboards and stairs where we were standing, but couldn't reproduce the sound. Another one was so loud that it prompted Mike to double check that all of the doors were locked. They were, and we were the only two people in the building.

The next experience was far more troubling, but fascinating. I was standing in front of an old-style bathroom, photographing a hair curling machine that looked to be a cross between the Medusa and a torture device. Mike was about twenty feet to my left in the hallway. I had just said something to him about the bizarre hair machine, when something touched my own hair.

I was wearing one of my Ghost Investigator baseball caps and it felt like a finger went into opening in the back and the under the hat. It moved back and forth once or twice, kind of playfully, and I froze like a statue.

"Mike, is there something touching the back of my head?" I asked, not wanting to freak out if I had merely backed into a coat rack or light fixture.

"No, there's nothing there. What's the matter?" he asked, wondering why I wasn't moving.

"Are you sure? Nothing is touching me?" I asked, with probably a bit more concern in my voice.

"There isn't anything behind you," he replied, coming over to where I stood.

The sensation stopped and I finally turned to have a look for myself. There was absolutely nothing that could have been touching me. In fact, there was open space as the servant's stairway was right there. A chill raced up my spine and I pulled off my hat to rub the lingering sensation out of my scalp. I had just said something about hair, when my own hair was touched. This appeared to be another example of, "I'm here and you know it!"

Just after taking this picture of the strange hair-curling machine,
someone touched my hair.

While I was having these very personal paranormal experiences, Mike was having some of his own. He kept complaining of a painful "stiff neck" which he said he had felt the moment he entered the building. This persisted and he couldn't understand what was wrong. I wondered out loud if there were any murders or suicides connected with this place. Then about an hour later, Mike discovered something that may have explained the pain in his neck.

We were getting some more equipment from the gear bags when he took a few steps away to look at the contents of a display case on the other side of a wall. It was tucked away in a dark corner and neither of us had noticed it before. Now Mike noticed, for sure, as his expression suddenly changed to one of surprise.

"Look at this!"

I walked over and was stunned to see a noose and shackles. As the display case was in the beautiful formal parlor with the curved seating area, this seemed to be an odd thing to put on display. Of course, it had to do with Pike County history—a very grisly piece of history. It was the actual noose used in the only execution hanging ever conducted in the county.

In 1896, Lizzie Schultz fled her abusive husband, Herman, in New York City, and found work in Wohlforth's High Point Farm in Shohola, Pennsylvania. He eventually found where she was staying and put a bullet in her head. (I just realized, that's two murders of people being shot in the head represented in adjoining rooms!) He had tried to make it look like a suicide, but a subsequent autopsy declared it to be murder, and he was tried and convicted—with his own sons testifying against him as to his violent temper and abuse of their mother.

But now it gets really strange—Lizzie's body had already been buried when the autopsy was ordered, so why bother exhuming the entire corpse when just the head would suffice? Her head was removed from her body, and the flesh was boiled off so that the skull could be examined. When it came time for Herman's execution, he requested that his wife's skull be buried with him! His request was denied.

Schultz had one other request—when the noose was placed tightly around his neck, he complained that the rope tickled and asked for it to be loosened. A little tickle was the least of his worries, however, as the loosened noose did not break his neck when the weight was released and he was "jerked into the air." Instead of an instant death, he very slowly suffocated to death.

And one more note: the execution took place in the tower of Milford's old court house, which still stands in the center of town. The building is said to be haunted, but that's another story...

The noose, and hand and ankle restraints used in Schultz's execution. To the right is the gun he used to murder his wife.

About 45 minutes into the investigation, Mike was on the second floor near the top of the staircase and I was several steps down. I heard a distinctive swishing sound, like a lady walking in a long taffeta dress. I closed my eyes and it was like I was suddenly whisked away to another time. I could clearly see the older woman with the upswept hair on the second floor. It wasn't like she was appearing in my reality, I had gone back to hers. So deep and consuming was this experience that I didn't know I was going down, literally—and the present, hard reality only returned when my rear end hit the stairs.

Mike saw me go down and rushed over to see if I was okay. I told him I was fine and explained—as best as I could—what had just transpired.

"Awesome!" he declared, appreciating the uniqueness of the experience as only a seasoned ghost investigator can.

If such an experience is awesome once, three times in one night is just incredible. A short time later when we were in the foyer, a cold chill swept over me and once again it was like some sci-fi time travel device had just been switched on. I sat down right on the floor—not because I felt dizzy or sick, but because I was so lost in the moment of another time I didn't trust my own two feet to keep me upright. Later, a similar experience hit Mike, and he, too, described it as being taken away to another time. Powerful stuff going on in this place…

The non-creepy basement proved to have a few surprises up its sleeve. As you enter the doorway, the corner directly to the left caught Mike's attention. He saw movement and when he turned to get a better look he saw a shadowy figure a little over five feet tall. It was visible for just a moment or two and was gone. As the lights were out and we were only using infrared it couldn't have been his body casting a shadow. And as I was sitting down on the other side of the room, I knew it couldn't be my shadow.

We tried coaxing this shy figure to reappear or make some sort of sound in the basement, but to no avail. Little did I realize, however, that I was about to get a paranormal earful. I was sitting in a chair in the center of the room when I "heard" the older woman again. It was like she was crying out in anguish, and I could clearly picture her leaning over the second floor banister with her arms outstretched. Mike noticed that I had suddenly whipped around in my seat as if I had heard something and he asked what had happened.

"It's like she's calling to me," I explained as best as I could under the circumstances. "She is on my brain. She really has my number!"

I was trying to convey the sense that she was coming in very loud and clear, and appeared to be directing cries for help at me. Needless to say, it was very distracting, to the point where I was starting to get a bit annoyed. I could hear her and see her, but what was I supposed to do about it?

The next thing that came through was the name Beatrice again. Only this time I was hearing a European pronunciation, *Bay-a-treech-a*. I don't suppose this is a typical frame of reference for a ghost hunter, but what came to mind was the great Italian poet, Dante, and his tragic lost love, Beatrice. I specifically recalled sitting in literature class hearing that name in Italian and thinking how beautiful it sounded, almost musical, so unlike the harsh anglicized version. Who knew my Masters in literature would come into play in the basement of a haunted mansion?

In any event, I had no idea why I kept hearing that name, and why I was hearing it in its foreign version. What I did know was that this woman was insistent and I couldn't shut her out, so we had to go to the staircase. I definitely did not want to go to the exact spot where I was seeing the woman by the banister, having learned my lesson the hard way in past cases—specifically the suicide case in Port Jervis. Instead, I sat on the stairs below and Mike sat a few steps above me. Unfortunately, I wasn't far enough away.

I could picture her bending over the banister reaching towards me, as if she wanted me to take her hands. I felt as if she was aware of the medical ordeal I had recently been through, and hoped she wasn't sensing something even more serious. It was very upsetting and I had to turn off the audio recorder to talk to Mike "off the record."

We discussed the situation and he asked if I wanted to leave. In truth, I wanted to run out as fast as I could, but I also wanted to see if I could work through this and get some answers. Considering the remarkable things that were about to happen I'm very glad I stayed, but trust me, it was very tough to stick it out.

"She knows I'm here," I told Mike, sensing that this unseen spirit could read me like a book. "She knows *me!*"

Suddenly the character of the woman changed completely—the anguished cries were silenced and outstretched arms were replaced by a figure gone limp, dejected, emotionally deflated and now dressed in all black. I assumed she had lost someone very dear to her, most likely her husband, and she then spent many years just sitting and staring off into space contemplating her loss. At least her focus had shifted away from me, but it was no less upsetting.

As Mike was fortunately spared any of this drama, I nonetheless wanted him to have some sign of her presence, lest he think I was really losing it. We asked for some outward sign that he could detect and there was a loud noise from downstairs, possibly from the Lincoln room. This time, Mike heard it. A few moments later, a mass of cold air came *up* the staircase—which is unusual since cold air is supposed to sink, not rise.

"Wow, I feel it!" Mike said, rubbing the goose bumps that had instantly arisen on his arms. "It's been hot the whole time we've been in here."

The arrow points to the spot on the second floor where I kept "seeing" the woman with the upswept hair and long dress.

We heard another knocking sound from below, so we decided to go back to the foyer. We noticed the chandelier in the curved parlor moving back and forth ever so slightly, but we could not rule out that our movement on the staircase had caused it, even though the place was built so solidly. We stood in the dark in silence for some time, but nothing happened. Then the woman returned.

"Oh no, she's back by the stairs!" I said, the exasperation in my voice clearly evident.

Reluctantly, we went back up the staircase and I braced myself for another emotional onslaught. Instead, I heard the distinctive swishing sound again just below me, as if a woman in a long dress was walking past the stairs towards the back of the house. I *knew* she wanted me to follow. Even though Mike and I had been working cases together for almost a decade, I felt like I was pushing the credibility envelope this night and really needed something to validate all of these experiences.

"There's something she wants me to find back there," I told Mike as I started running down the stairs to follow the swishing sound.

To my initial disappointment, the sounds led to the back office with its computers and copying machine—not exactly the type of things that could validate that a woman who had been dead for about a hundred years knew who I was. Still, I searched the walls for any kind of photos or documents, not having a clue about what I was looking for, but willing to bet anything that something was there for me to find.

Just as I was about to give up, Mike pointed behind me and said, "What about those?"

I turned to see a row of large file cabinets. Could the thing the woman wanted me to find be in there? I randomly opened a drawer to see what was inside and found hanging folders packed with newspaper clippings and articles. If every drawer was as filled as this one, there had to be thousands of pieces of paper, any one of which could contain my validation. I could spend a year going through these file cabinets, how was I ever going to find what I was looking for in one night? As it turned out, I didn't even need ten minutes.

I found the "C" drawer that contained several dated folders labeled "The Columns" and just pulled one out marked 2003-2006. I was crouching on the floor with the folder and my flashlight, intently focused on my search when Mike commented, "You look like a burglar. You know, we could turn the lights on."

Perhaps I had been a little *too* focused.

Mike switched on the lights, which made things a lot easier, and I continued to scan through clippings and articles. Then one caught

Mike took this infrared photo of me looking "like a burglar,"
feverishly scanning files in the dark.

my eye that had the magic word—ghost—and upon closer
inspection I saw that it was a newspaper story from the *Pike County
Courier* about haunted places in the Milford area. It had been
printed in October of 2008, so it was actually misfiled and had I
specifically been looking for it I wouldn't have found it. It didn't
cross my mind that this was what I was looking for, but I started to
read it as I was simply interested in other haunted locations in the
area. Then my eyes wandered to a list of recommended websites at
the end of the article.

There was *www.ghostinvestigator.com* at the top of the list, and
I must confess that in my semi-oblivious state I didn't immediately
recognize that it was *my* website. Then it hit me. I jumped up and
put the article in front of Mike and pointed to the list. I have rarely
seen Mike be at a loss for words, but this was definitely one of those
times.

What caught my eye: My website at the top of the list.

He stared at the newspaper clipping for a few moments without saying anything, then asked in amazement, "How did you get on there?"

"I think she wanted to let me know that she knows who I am," I replied, my head whirling in a heady combination of shock and exhilaration.

"But...ah...eh..."

"You can't even talk," I said laughing.

Then simultaneously we declared, "What are the chances?"

I turned to get my camera to take pictures of the article when Mike shocked me even further.

"Here's your name! It says *Linda Zimmermann, a paranormal expert*," he said, pointing to the most glaring part of the validation I had missed!

of orbs in each of the rooms. Linda Zimmerman, a paranormal expert visited the museum and confirmed many of the sightings.

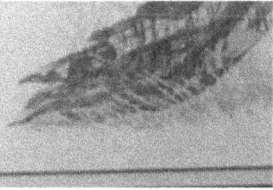

Mike spotted my name in the article...proof that the spirit knew who I was!

So there it was: I sense this woman repeatedly trying to communicate with me, leading me into the office for proof that she is a conscious spirit who knew who I was, and then within minutes I find the one article among thousands that has my name on it, referring to me as someone who researches ghosts!

This is all so far "out there" that I wouldn't dare write something like this in my fiction, because it would be too unbelievable! Hopefully at that moment, any questions Mike may have had about my experiences were answered. And truthfully, my own considerable doubts were also dispelled.

Now I want everyone to take a moment to digest this before I continue on to the next part of the story…Okay, are you ready for this? Remember I kept hearing the name Beatrice from the time I first walked in the building? Later in the evening Mike and I were walking down the second floor hallway, which is directly behind the spot where I kept envisioning the woman. He was looking at what was hanging on the walls, and his flashlight stopped in a particular spot.

"Linda, you have to see this!"

I took a look at the wooden framed collection of photos, and my jaw dropped at the caption up top: "Phebe Davis Bailey and her daughter Beatrice"!

Always looking for the rational explanation, I thought that perhaps when we first took our quick walkthrough of the place that I saw this caption without registering it, a kind of subliminal message that stuck in my head. I suggested this possibility to Mike, but he recalled that I brought up the name Beatrice as soon as we arrived, *before going upstairs*—and it couldn't have been a subliminal message if I hadn't even been on the second floor yet! Also, I kept hearing a foreign pronunciation of the name, which may help to tie together this whole crazy night.

The following is a compilation of information gathered from the museum staff and several articles, and how it may apply to our experiences.

It has been suggested by witnesses and psychics that the primary spirit who haunts The Columns is Madame Juliette Pierce, the wife of the famous philosopher and scientist, Charles Sanders Pierce, the founder of the study of the philosophy of pragmatism. Charles died in 1914, twenty years before Juliette's passing. The Pierces had lived in a home called Arisbe, about a quarter of a mile away from The Columns. While Juliette never lived in this house, many of her belongings were donated to the museum, including her black mourning clothes.

Juliette was something of an enigma, as her past is shrouded in mystery before she met Mr. Pierce in New York City. Some claim she was a gypsy somewhere in Europe, others say she was a descendant of the poet Jean Froissart and was born in Nancy, France, and she had once mentioned playing with Kaiser Wilhelm when they were children. In any event, she had clearly come from

Europe with enough money to support herself, and became a devoted supporter of her husband and his work. Of special note to a ghost investigator, her obituary also states that she was "well known for reading fortunes by the cards," so she may have been psychically gifted. (Legend has it that the antique set of cards she used had foretold the downfall of Napoleon.)

A photo of Juliette and Charles Pierce in The Columns collection.
Juliette's hair is *exactly* how I pictured it on the woman I "saw."

So, what conclusions, or at least speculations, can be drawn from this information? If it was indeed Madame Pierce who was trying to communicate, the images of her in anguish and then as a woman in mourning fit the profile of a grieving widow. Also, being from Europe, her pronunciation of the name Beatrice would have been different than the way we say it today. I don't think the spirit of Beatrice is in the house—although anything is possible—I simply think that it was Juliette's way of validating that she was on that second floor in the hallway and by the banister. And as for leading me to find my own name in the file cabinets, well, she is one clever spirit who obviously has some clever psychic tricks up her puffy sleeves!

***Okay, stop the presses for some breaking news. After completing the last paragraph, I stopped writing to call Lori Strelecki, the director at The Columns, for more information about the original owners of the house (that section of this story had not yet been written), and to ask if there was any opera connections, as it was one of the things I sensed upon entering the house.

When Mike had noticed the pictures of Beatrice, we also saw on the opposite wall a stunning portrait of a beautiful woman in a yellow gown who was obviously singing. I asked Lori about this portrait, by local artist John Newton Howitt, and she told me it was Diedre Aselford, an opera singer who once lived in Milford and went on to great success in Europe!

Then came even more remarkable news. The historical society had just hosted an event the previous weekend, and Lori noticed a woman with long black hair who had been walking around the place for hours and wondered what she was doing there for so long. Finally, the woman approached her and with some hesitation said there was something she had to tell her: There is a woman named Juliette who inhabits the second floor in the hallway from the back room to the staircase!

I kid you not—I had just written that exact thing, and minutes later come to find that someone else had the exact experience. I have absolutely no doubt now about what transpired that night: the spirit of Juliette Pierce is on that second floor and she told me about Beatrice and an opera connection so I would know exactly where she was. I know, it all sounds fantastic, and this newly-honed psychic ability will take some getting used to for me, but there it is in one incredible paranormal nutshell, and I will be willing to swear an oath in court that this is what happened.

Now back to our regularly scheduled story…

It almost seems anticlimactic to continue with the rest of the results of our investigation, but there are still some experiences to relate on the third floor. There were several odd sounds on this floor that could best be described as popping sounds, and there were also footsteps. One instance of the sounds of footsteps and movement was so loud and close behind me I spun around quickly—and almost backed right into Mike—but saw nothing. The predominant experience, however, was that persistent sense of annoyance, as if someone up there very much wanted us to get lost. This was their domain, and they didn't take kindly to intruders. This was the one section of the house where Mike was genuinely uncomfortable and we didn't spend as much time on this floor as we did on the others. We know when we aren't wanted!

We decided to pack it up for the night, and once we disengaged from investigation mode we both realized how exhausted we were. As I have said in the past, even if nothing happens during an investigation, the mere act of being on constant high alert for several hours is very taxing. Combine that with all we experienced that night with the resultant adrenaline rushes, and we were two worn out ghost investigators.

So, do I think The Columns in Milford, Pennsylvania is haunted? Without a doubt!

And is the spirit of Madame Juliette Pierce there, still trying to convey her grief and anguish at the loss of her brilliant husband, for whom she tirelessly exhibited support? Also, there is no doubt in my mind.

There may be many others there as well, such as the decidedly anti-social spirit on the third floor. Perhaps there are also certain energies connected with the Lincoln flag and Civil War artifacts that may not generate actual apparitions, but could provide impressions to those who are sensitive. And let us not forget that this museum has a noose used to hang a murderer!

Despite this paranormal bounty of the bizarre, I must stress we never felt threatened at any point, and at no time sensed any menacing entities. Also, as there are employees who have worked in the building for years and have never encountered anything unusual, you should not hesitate to visit The Columns if you are skittish about getting up close and personal with ghosts.

The Columns is worth a visit if only for the Lincoln flag. Then there are all the other Civil War artifacts, furnishings, architecture, original clothing, special exhibits, etc., all in a magnificent structure in a beautiful town. And on top of all that there are the ghosts, so what are you waiting for?

One final note: If you do visit The Columns and encounter Madame Pierce on the second floor, just tell her I sent you—she knows who I am...

Mike's infrared photo of me on the stairs at the start of the investigation, as my attention is immediately drawn to the woman by the banister above me.

Infrared photo courtesy of Michael Worden.

Body language and expression says it all: Although my attention is riveted to the spirit reaching out to me from the banister, I'm pressed against the wall of the staircase trying to put as much distance as possible between us. Ghost hunting often tests your comfort level, and the energetic and persistent Madame Pierce was certainly pushing the envelope that night.

Cliff Park
Milford, PA

It's hard enough for us to picture what America was like as far back as the time of the Revolutionary War. Try to imagine, then, what life was like here in 1627, the year that England granted 300,000 acres of land in the "New World" to the Buchanans. Part of that huge grant included land in Milford, Pennsylvania, where the charming Cliff Park Inn stands today amongst the silence of thousands of acres of beautiful old growth forest.

Well, maybe it isn't totally silent. There are the songs of a few hundred species of birds and the occasional soulful call of a wolf. Then there are the unexplained sounds of footsteps, doors opening, and furniture being moved—where no living people are present. But that's all part of the charm here, as the place is so peaceful and restful that even the dead come back to stay!

The Buchanan clan did well in its new country, with one of its members, James, becoming the 15th President of the United States, 1857-1861. It was James' uncle who owned Cliff Park, and as a boy the future president spent summers here. Another member of the family went from this Milford house to the White House—Harriet Lane, James' young niece, acted as First Lady during his administration, as he was the only chief executive to never marry.

In 1814, a humble one-room cabin—in which nine people lived!—was expanded to a spacious farm house. Over the years there were several other additions, including the Victorian-era porch and Cypress Room dining area, as well as the construction of numerous out buildings. Arguably, the greatest change to the property came in the 1920s when Cliff Park House was opened as an inn, and the golf course was added. Remarkably, this historic site is on the national register not because of the house, but because of its golf course! The 9-hole USGA course was the first in the country to allow women, and it was also the first to be owned and developed by a woman.

That tradition of capable and resourceful women at Cliff Park continues today with owner Stephanie Brown, who manages to successfully juggle the operations of the B&B, restaurant, sports bar, golf course, catering, weddings, and a host of special events. It's her work ethic and philosophy that allow guests the ability to be as active as they wish, or to be completely inactive and do nothing but rest and relax. However, even Stephanie admits there are some things she just can't schedule—such as the paranormal activity.

There appears to be quite a long roster of ghosts, and if you plan to stay here you might want to keep a scorecard of all the various personalities and their activities. The following is a sampling of the many spirits of Cliff Park:

> **The Lady in Brown**: If you feel a rush of air coming down the main staircase, keep an eye open for the Lady in Brown. Her dress and hair place her in the 1920s, and her appearances always follow the same pattern. Many witnesses have seen her coming down the staircase, going out the front door, walking across the porch onto the lawn and through the stone pillars, continuing through the woods to the edge of the 900-

foot cliff overlooking the Delaware River, then disappearing. Speculation centers on her being part of the crew for one of the silent movies filmed here in the 1910s and 20s. Perhaps some movie star or producer jilted her and drove her to commit suicide by leaping off the cliff? Attempts to search for records of her death have so far been unsuccessful, but such a tragedy would no doubt have been hushed up, as who would want an ugly suicide connected with an innocent Mary Pickford film?

The staircase where the Lady in Brown is seen and felt.

- **Getting Juiced by Uncle Stew**: Uncle Stew was a Buchanan, and is still a great protector of the family property. If you see a man wearing a plaid flannel shirt, it's Uncle Stew. And if a can of juice comes flying at your head, that's also an indication that Uncle Stew is nearby. But let me explain, lest you cancel your reservations upon reading this. Every business has to deal with some bad employees who may steal, do drugs, etc., but it's difficult to catch them in the act and find grounds to fire them. Enter the champion of good, Uncle Stew, combating the forces of evil, the bad employees. There is a set of cabinets in the kitchen which used to contain large cans of juice. One day a bad employee was standing fifteen feet away from the cabinets when the doors suddenly swung open and a very large can of tomato juice flew through the air and struck him in the head! Another bad employee was peppered with small cans of pineapple juice, which also traveled through the air over fifteen feet. Another miscreant had a rack of ladles fall on him every day, even though no other employees had any problems with the ladles. There was no need to fire these bad employees, as Stew convinced them to leave.

- **Fanny** was a former employee who must have had quite a sweet tooth, as it has followed her into death. If anyone leaves candy or chocolates out, chances are you will find them gone a short time later, with the wrappers strewn all about. (If an employee or guest was pilfering the candy, it is doubtful they would leave behind the telltale evidence of the wrappers all over the floor.)

- **Sally** may be the most active spirit here. She was housekeeper of the estate for 50 years and died in the 1920s. But even death isn't keeping the ever-diligent Sally from doing her job of making sure that everyone else does their jobs. If lights are left on or something is

The kitchen cabinets that used to hold the cans of juice
that Stew liked to throw.

not closed properly for the night, Sally will move furniture creating quite a racket—and has even been known to throw a chair! Things will only quiet down once everything is done right. She has been seen as a glowing form or floating light. Her small bedroom is now part of the expanded guest room #10, which not surprisingly may be the most active room in the house. Don't be surprised if upon entering room #10 you find an imprint on the bed as if someone is lying down. Turn your back for a moment and then look again, and the bedspread will be smoothed out. Sally likes to be treated with respect, so it's a good idea to greet her politely upon entering her former bedroom, and don't forget to thank her for her hospitality.

> **Walt** was the golf course manager whose gruff personality has also carried over to the other side. He doesn't like change, and will display his displeasure in the form of making door locks stick to keep certain people out, and also throwing things, which seems to be a popular pastime for the spirits of Cliff Park.

> **The child of the 3rd floor** is often heard giggling and running up and down the halls, particularly near room #14. One day an employee's 10-year-old daughter was exploring the building and when she came downstairs she asked who the little girl was on the third floor. There weren't any other children in the house that day. Renovations in that section of the building revealed old wallpaper that indicated it was once the nursery.

> **Annie,** the woman who developed the golf course, has been seen in various locations, particularly on the porch and greens.

> **"Big George"** still helps out in the kitchen.

> **The doorknob to the closet behind the hostess station** often rattles and the door opens on its own. Some suspect Walt is behind this activity.

> **Room #9** may have the creepiest phenomena— children's hand prints appear on a recessed section of wall. The wall has even been re-plastered, but the small hand prints returned. Numerous coats of paint have been applied, but the paint always peels, just at that spot, and the hand prints always return within several weeks. They finally had to hang a picture over the spot. People standing outside have often seen

lights moving around the room and have heard odd sounds.

The alcove in Room #9 where the child's hand print appears.
(Infrared photo.)

➢ **A young woman**, described as being about 19 years old, has been seen in various places throughout the inn.

➢ **Room #11** has a decorative ladder that moves. Stephanie and staff members will place the ladder against the dresser, only to find it against the same spot on the wall the next morning.

The ladder that moves on its own in Room #11.

> **The bar in the Cypress Room** has a large shelf bolted to the wall to hold the bottles of liquor. One day the bartender took a step to enter the adjacent kitchen door, when the heavy shelf came crashing off the wall, missing him by inches. He no longer works there. (Could Uncle Stew have been behind this, too?)

The bar that came off the wall and narrowly missed an employee.

> **Windows in the guest rooms** open by themselves. Many guests have reported waking up in the middle of the night and finding their windows wide open, and they were certain they were closed when they went to sleep.

> **Sports Bar** patrons have reported many strange occurrences over the years. However, given the very nature of a sports bar, these alcohol-tainted accounts would not be admissible in a paranormal court of law!

It was a cool and rainy spring evening when my husband Bob, Mike Worden, and I arrived at the Cliff Park Inn. The first thing we noticed was the tranquil setting; the second was how deceptive the exterior of the building is, as it is much more expansive inside than we first thought. Stephanie greeted us and gave us a very informative and entertaining tour, explaining both the history and the mysteries of the place.

We naturally wanted to concentrate on the areas of the most activity—the kitchen, dining rooms, and guest rooms #9 and #10—but we wanted to cover the entire inn, if possible. Stephanie graciously gave us free rein, except for room #5, which was occupied for the evening.

My plan was to first photograph all of the rooms on the main floor. As I stood in the parlor that was once the old one-room cabin and held up the camera, the floor lamp right next to me turned on and off, twice! *Okay*, I thought, *this is too good to be true already*.

"Uh, Mike?" I called out calmly, not wanting to jump to any conclusions. "Something might have already happened."

He was in the adjacent main living room getting equipment ready, and came in and asked what had occurred. I told him about the lamp and he said he had tried some switches in the other room, but why should they control a light in this room? Of course, we had to check it out, so he went back into the living room and sure enough, one of the switches controlled the lamp next to me. Mystery solved, unfortunately, as it would have made a great part of the story!

Even though there was nothing paranormal about it, I wanted to relate this episode to emphasize the importance of examining everything on an investigation with a critical eye. I could have jumped up and down and claimed a ghost turned a light on and off—and believe me I was tempted—but I made sure to immediately look for a rational explanation. It may be disappointing to discover that what at first seems to be great evidence is not, but if you are serious about your investigations *you* have to be *your strongest skeptic*.

My disappointment was quite brief, as my K2 meter's indicator lights came on when I approached the chair in the corner of the room. Stephanie told us that she often spends the night sleeping in this chair and has felt breezes and cold spots moving around it. I

The parlor chair where there were high EMF readings.

couldn't attest to that, but the meter certainly indicated there was an electromagnetic field around the chair, and I couldn't find a natural source for it.

Bob and Mike started scanning the whole main floor for EMF and found a strong, consistent field along the front wall of the house. Perhaps there are electrical wires in the walls, but are they in every section of wall, running the length of the house? We had to chalk this up as interesting, but not definitive.

While camcorders were set up and left running in rooms #9 and #10, we began a systematic investigation of all the other guest rooms. Our first stop was room #8. Bob and I sat down on a bench seat, while Mike stood on the other side of the bed. The room was a comfortable temperature when we entered, but I quickly began feeling an icy chill, to the point where I was soon shivering and had the distinct feeling that a female presence was the culprit.

"Is there a woman in here with us?" I asked, and then said to Bob and Mike, "I'm hearing the word *floral* for some reason."

We looked around the room, but it was not decorated in a floral motif. As I was saying that *floral* just didn't make any sense, I actually felt a somewhat indignant reprimand—something along the lines of a slightly more polite version of, "Not *floral*, you idiot, *FLORA*!"

I immediately said out loud that I had been corrected, that the woman was saying Flora. The instant I spoke her name, the K2 lights came on as if to signify that this time I had gotten it right. We proceeded to have a Q&A with Flora, and what emerged was a woman from the earlier years of the house, who wanted to particularly emphasize something about the family into which she had married. I felt very strongly about this issue, that it was something of significance and would help identify her (along with a portrait that existed somewhere), although I admit I had no clue as to whether she was proud of marrying into the Buchanan family, or had been a Buchanan who had made an advantageous marital connection to an even more prominent family.

Let me skip ahead now to the break we took about an hour later. Flora was still very much on my mind when we came across Stephanie in the living room. I felt kind of silly asking her, as I don't claim to be a psychic per se, but perhaps I was emboldened by my two validated intuitive experiences at The Columns just the week before.

"Do you know of anyone named Flora connected with this house?" I asked Stephanie, fully expecting her to say she had never heard of anyone here by that name.

"Why yes!" she replied, to my utter astonishment. Bob and Mike looked at Stephanie, then at me, with expressions of great surprise. "Flora was one of the Buchanans who always wanted it known that she had *married up* into the Quinn family."

I processed this startling information for a few moments and then asked, "Is there a portrait of her somewhere?"

"Yes," Stephanie quickly replied. "The current Mr. Buchanan has a portrait of Flora."

I once again got strange looks from Bob and Mike, and I no doubt had an equal look of amazement on my face.

So there it was, two psychic bull's eyes in a week. It wasn't as if I had picked some common name like Mary, of which there could have been dozens over the course of two centuries. I had clearly heard the name of the one and only Flora who felt great pride in a socially upgraded position through marriage, and whose portrait could confirm her identity. Someday I would certainly like to get a look at this woman who had gotten into my head...

Mike took this infrared photo of Bob and I in Room #8. As you can see, I was encountering a cold spot. Could it have been the presence of Flora?

There were completely different thoughts when we entered room #9. To me, it had the residue of a death. I heard the words "watery demise," but wasn't sure if it was from a drowning in the traditional sense, or an illness which filled the lungs with fluid, perhaps pneumonia. I commented to Bob and Mike about the cheery thoughts I was having.

We took some photos of the room, paying particular attention to the alcove where the children's hand prints appear. While shooting in infrared in the dark room, I thought I saw something in front of me through the viewfinder. I took three quick pictures of the alcove, and while reviewing them the next day I noticed that an oddly-shaped, dark shadow appeared in the first two, but not in the third. I immediately emailed them to Mike and asked if he had been directly behind me with his infrared camera, which could mean that the shape I had photographed was probably nothing more than my own shadow.

We studied all of our photos from that room, and while he had been behind me, he was to my right so the angles were not correct for the size and position of the shadow being cast slightly to my right. He would have had to be directly behind me or to my left, and his infrared light would have had to be on at that moment. Still, even though we couldn't adequately explain it, I am leaning towards this being nothing more than my own shadow, but I honestly can't say what it was with any certainty.

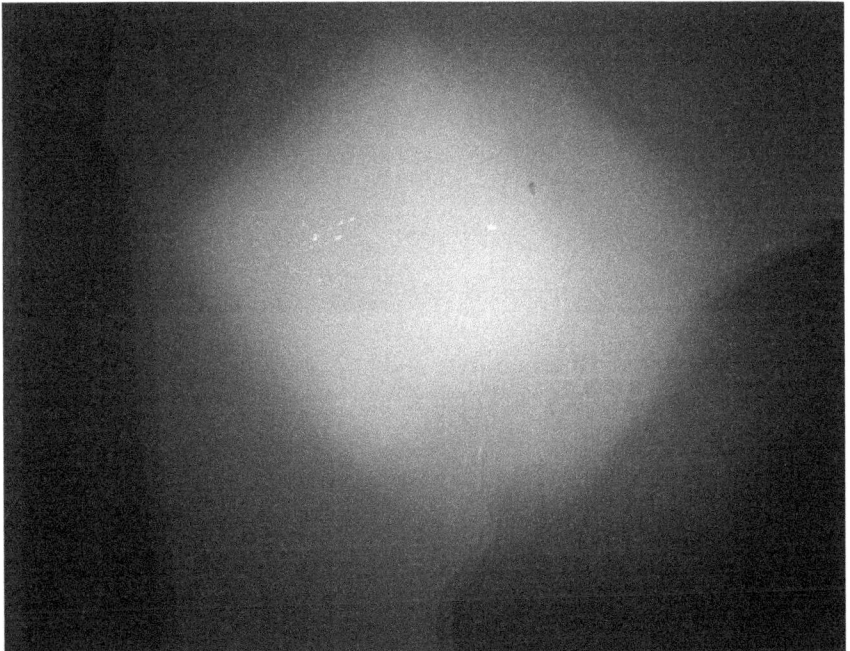

The bright diamond shape is from my camera's infrared light.
Is the dark shape on the right my own shadow?

We sat quietly in the darkness for several minutes, with nothing occurring. There wasn't even the slightest flicker on the K2 meters, one of which rested on my leg, the other about ten feet away on the bed in front of Mike. Then there was the sound of someone moving around somewhere outside of the room, but as there were guests in #5, it was certainly possible the sounds were coming from them. As a test, Mike asked that whoever it was bang on something to give us a sign. Immediately there was a noise *inside* the room.

When I asked if the person had been a servant, the K2 meter on my leg lit up to the yellow light and I felt an electric jolt.

"Whoa!" I said in surprise as the intense tingling sensation coursed through my body. "I feel like I'm sitting on an electric grid. I am *buzzing* with energy!"

Bob and Mike were so busy looking at the lights on my meter, they didn't notice that the meter right in front of Mike also was lit up to the yellow light. Whatever had suddenly entered the room was powerful enough to create a strong electromagnetic field, not to mention make me feel like I was plugged into an electrical outlet—and it all started when I said the word "servant."

An image of this female servant flashed past my mind's eye: dressed in a white uniform similar to that of a nurse, very prim and proper, exceedingly fastidious—in other words, a perfectionist who took her work very seriously.

Bob scanned the room from floor to ceiling with a more sensitive meter to see how widespread the EM field was, and remarkably, the only measurable fields were around the K2 meters...or was it just around Mike and I? If the readings had somehow been from electrical wiring in the walls, surely the EM field would extend the distance from the wall to our meters—not be totally absent for several feet than suddenly manifest in two unique spots in the room. I definitely have to assign this activity to something else manifesting!

We next went to room #10, making sure we thanked Sally for allowing us to enter. Mike even said that she shouldn't worry, as we wouldn't be sitting on *her* bed. The reason he said this was because of a story Stephanie told us about a group trying to conduct a ghost hunt there. She found one of the male members of the group lying on Sally's bed telling her to come and give them a sign, but hadn't gotten any results for over an hour.

"Are you surprised?" Stephanie asked. "You are a strange man lying on a lady's bed demanding that she join you! Can you blame her for keeping her distance?"

The man admitted that he hadn't thought about it that way and quickly stood up. Stephanie proceeded to smooth out the covers and fluff Sally's pillows, and the team's meters suddenly "started going crazy." Remember boys and girls, it pays to be polite, even to the dead!

While we didn't get any sounds or readings inside Sally's room, we all clearly heard someone walking in the hallway just outside the room. We listened for a minute to make sure there was no mistake and then opened the door. The sounds stopped and no one was there. This was one incident of footsteps we could not attribute to the guests in room #5, unless they possessed the power of invisibility, of course.

Rooms #1 and #2 proved to be very interesting. At first in #2 there were absolutely no EMF readings, then suddenly they were very high—a phenomena that repeated throughout the building all night long. Bob and I went into room #1 (the doors of the two rooms face one another) and Mike was standing in the hall between the two rooms taking pictures, when he heard the door handle of room #2 start to rattle. Then there were more sounds of footsteps going down the hall. It was as if whatever was giving off the EMF readings in room #2 had exited and walked down the hall. We all stood in the hallway for a while and heard the sounds of creaking floorboards and movement both in front and behind us for several minutes. Unfortunately, we were never able to see or photograph who was making those sounds.

Our plan was to investigate the kitchen next. As Stephanie and I entered the kitchen we heard a loud banging noise, and we assumed it was a waitress who had come upstairs from the sports bar. However, she was nowhere to be seen, and there was no response when Stephanie called out her name through a couple of doorways. I was beginning to think we had heard something unusual, until I saw that the water in two of the three bins used to soak dirty dishes was swirling, as if someone had recently dropped in a couple of plates. Even though the waitress was nowhere to be found, the observation of the dish bin water made me conclude that the sounds might have had a rational explanation.

Mike in the hallway by Rooms #1 and #2.

As I said, our plan was to investigate the kitchen, but the noise from all the refrigerators, freezers, dishwashers, ice maker, etc., coupled with the high EMF readings they generated made it kind of pointless. And we weren't about the ask Stephanie to cut the power, so we moved on to the dining rooms.

Again, Bob and Mike were hot on the trail of high EMF readings in the Cypress Room, trying to determine their origin. This went on for several minutes as they slowly walked back and forth across the room. Then suddenly, the readings were gone. If there is a natural explanation for readings to come and go like that, I would love to hear it!

Stephanie, Bob, and Mike search for the
source of the EMF readings in the dining area.

Our investigation of the Cliff Park Inn that night did lack one thing, good weather! As we were unable to get any exterior shots or walk the grounds in the pouring rain, Mike and I arranged to return on a sunny day, which during the cool, wet spring of 2009 were unfortunately few and far between. It took about a week to get a nice day, so we took full advantage, and after taking pictures of the inn, headed for the wooded trails.

I have to say, as someone who loves the woods and loves to hike, these were some of the most beautiful trails I've had the pleasure of walking. There's a wonderful variety of towering trees, plants, birds, and other wildlife. Then before you know it, you come upon scenic overlooks along the cliffs with absolutely breathtaking views of the Delaware River valley and the surrounding hills. I can't imagine how stunning these vistas are during the fall foliage season, or on a clear, crisp winter's day with a snow-covered landscape.

At the risk of sounding like a travel brochure, the woods and the view alone are worth a visit to Cliff Park. Bring a picnic lunch and make sure you have a hefty memory card for your camera, because you are going to want to take some time to explore the cliff views, woods, lake, and wildlife. We did not see the Lady in Brown during our hike, but I wasn't disappointed, as the day was perfect even without ghosts!

One of the magnificent views from the cliffs.

Did the mysterious Lady in Brown jump from these cliffs?

So what is my overall assessment of the inn and grounds at Cliff Park? Based upon the numerous eyewitness accounts over the years and our own experiences, I would have to say this is one of the most haunted places I've visited. However, how this place sets itself apart from other extremely haunted locations is that there doesn't appear to be any malevolent spirits here. (You can't include the juice can episodes, as Uncle Stew was just trying to protect his home.)

One thing Stephanie said really stuck in my mind: Even employees who have been fired keep coming back to the inn to spend time and enjoy the tranquil setting. If the living refuse to leave, how can we persuade the dead to move on?

So, whether you are looking for a peaceful rest, or to rest in peace, the Cliff Park Inn is the place to be!

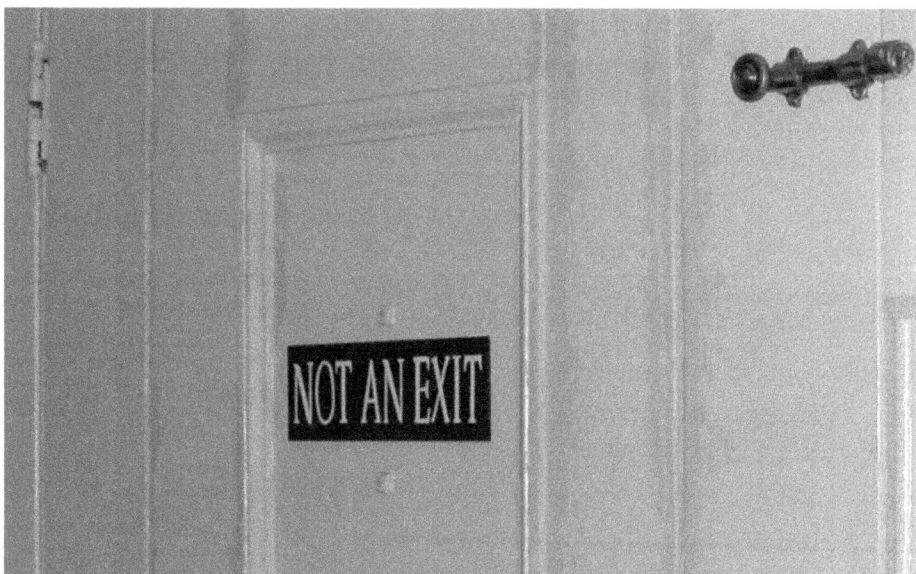

This sign on one of the doors may be more appropriate than they know, as no one seems to want to leave the Cliff Park Inn.

Cliff Park Inn
155 Cliff Park Road, Milford, PA 18337
Reservations: (800)225-6535
www.cliffparkinn.com
escape@cliffparkinn.com

Tamarack Lodge
Greenfield Park, New York

"You'll Never Want to Leave"
　　　　　　　　-text on the back of Tamarack postcards

"This place is alive with dead people, a literal ghost town."

Those were the words I spoke into my digital recorder one night in October of 2008 during an investigation at the derelict Tamarack Lodge in Greenfield Park, New York. What began as a modest boarding house in 1927, became a sprawling resort in the post-WWII years, part of the famous Jewish "Borscht Belt" of the Catskills.

Entertainers the likes of Jerry Lewis and Danny Kaye kept audiences laughing, while rock legends like Cream, The Who, and Janis Joplin shook the rafters. It was a place for families to spend their summer vacations away from the heat of New York City, but it was also the scene of steamy singles weekends.

Regardless of your taste in comedians and music, or your moral convictions about swinging singles, the activities at the Tamarack appear at first glance to be harmless fun, and certainly not fodder for hauntings. After all, resorts are places for people to relax, eat, and get rejuvenated. They certainly aren't places where people die...or are they?

In reality, the number of fatalities over the decades is stunning—an estimated 157! My ghost hunting partner, Detective Mike Worden, puts it all into perspective:

"We have to remember that the Tamarack (like the other resorts) was a small city with thousands of guests and employees on any given day. Deaths by natural causes, accidents, illness, and even suicide and homicide, would not be uncommon or unexpected. Even the alleged number of 157 deaths is not, in my opinion, unreasonable considering that over the course of many decades tens of thousands of guests stayed there."

I am reminded of a case years ago in which an older woman had died at a wedding reception. At the time, I was shocked to find out just how many people actually die at such events—the direct result of older folks partying a little too hard. Such must also be the case at resorts, especially those catering to the senior set. We must also not forget the younger generation doing too many drugs, people of all ages having accidents, or even those more sinister forms of death. There was supposedly at least one murder committed at the resort. In 1957, one of the cooks killed his allegedly unfaithful wife with a hatchet.

Any single death can leave an imprint on a site, if not an active spirit, so 157 deaths would most likely leave quite a mark. I was anxious to investigate the Tamarack and its alleged bevy of ghosts, but regrettably I was unable to go when Barbara Bleitzhofer arranged a date in the summer of 2008. Mike was able to make it, though, and I eagerly awaited his report the next day. Unfortunately, I was surprised and disappointed to hear that nothing happened. Had it not been for Barb's previous experiences, I may not have gone on the second investigation, and what a night I would have missed!

When Mike and I arrived that chilly night, we met up with Barbara and her friend Duane Smith, who had both been there several times and knew their way around. That was a very good thing, as the place was a confusing sprawl of buildings and it would have taken Mike and I half the night trying to figure out where we were. We used the large theater area to unpack all our gear and wasted no time getting down to business. As we "geared up," Barbara told us that a young girl has been seen on the stage—perhaps some poor, little lost soul still looking for stardom?

Before beginning the investigation, Mike explored the control room of the theater.

One of our first stops, and the first place we encountered anything unusual, was at a long soda fountain/bar not far from the lobby. Barb and I were behind the bar with our K-2 meters, which have a series of lights ranging from green, to yellow, to red to indicate the relative strength of electromagnetic fields. When I asked if anyone wanted to give us a sign, the yellow light on my meter instantly lit up, while Barb's went full red. A second or two later the lights went out, but lit up again as we asked other questions.

Mike brought over his digital EMF meter and was able to confirm the coming and going of a substantial EM field. We searched for a natural explanation, but couldn't find any active electrical source from the bar equipment or outlets. Even if we had, that would not have accounted for the field appearing and disappearing, seemingly in response to our questions.

So, not even five minutes into our investigation of the Tamarack, we had a definite point of interest. Little did we realize that it was just the tiny tip of the paranormal iceberg in this vast ghost town.

We worked our way outside and over to the bungalow section. One of the odd and unsettling things about the Tamarack is that you can walk into one room and find the beds made and everything looking as though it was ready for guests, then turn the corner and find decay and rubble. The latter was the case in this bungalow area, and while stepping over collapsed pieces of buildings can be a tricky and dangerous proposition in the dark, in this instance it provided a moment of comic relief.

"Mike, could you get the door for us?" I asked, as if nothing was out of the ordinary.

However, this door had been torn from its hinges and was lying on the floor blocking the entrance. Mike played the scene perfectly, calmly picking it up and tossing it to one side with the demeanor of a gentleman opening the door for two ladies entering a fine restaurant. Barb and I thanked him politely, then proceeded to crunch over the remaining debris and broken glass with our hiking boots. Ghost hunting chivalry is not dead!

Things really got interesting in the Westchester building, where despite a lot of broken windows, many of the rooms looked as though the maid service had just been through. I asked for a sign from anyone wishing to communicate, and there was an immediate beep from a smoke detector somewhere down the hall, followed by

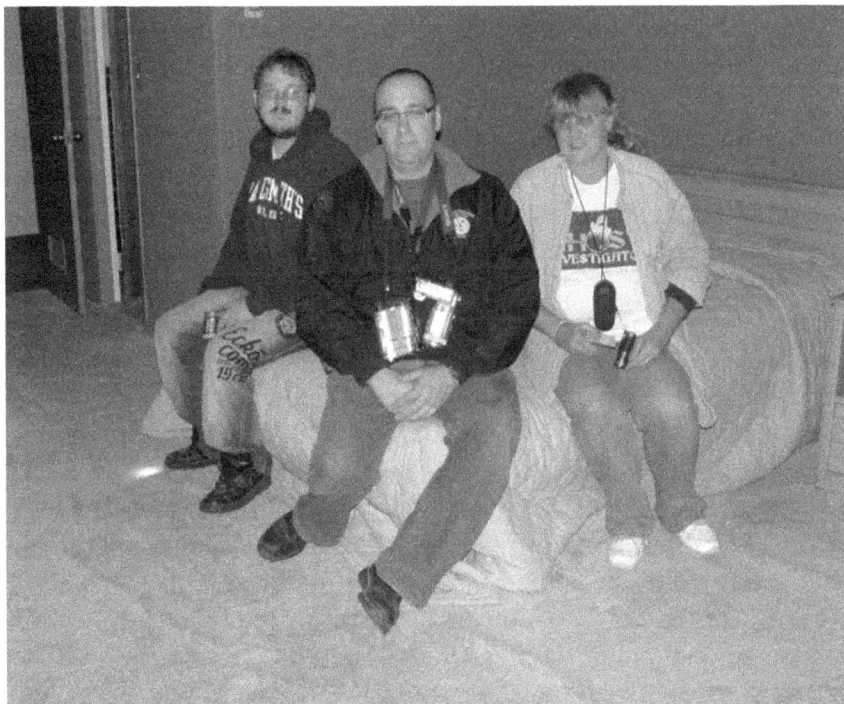

Duane, Mike, and Barbara in a room that looked as though the maid had just finished making the bed. In the hallway just beyond this room, the ceiling and walls are crumbling.

some other inexplicable noises of movement. I was surprised any batteries in this place were still functioning after being closed for so many years, but certainly didn't consider the beeping to be anything paranormal.

However, when I reviewed the audio recordings at a later date I discovered that for the entire time that we were in the Westchester building the smoke detector only beeped twice, with the second time occurring exactly as the first: I asked for another sign and there was an immediate beep, followed by other noises that sounded like someone moving around.

I had to reconsider my earlier assumption. If spirits can affect all manner of electrical devices, why couldn't they make a smoke detector beep? I wish now that I had found that detector and checked to see if it even had a battery in it. At the very least, this was all something to keep in mind for future investigations—never assume something is normal or paranormal without considering all the evidence.

An infrared photo of a hallway in the Westchester building.

In addition to the inexplicable noises around us in the dark, things were heating up in other ways, and quite literally. Barb experienced an unusual hot spot, which she described as being like that blast of heat you get at the door of a department store in the winter. Duane was able to confirm a ten to fifteen degree difference in temperature in the area where Barb stood. She also began to feel as if she was being followed, perhaps by a former maintenance man. Meanwhile, I was getting the disturbing sense that many spirits were starting to gather around us, and Mike said more than once that the atmosphere was completely different from his first investigation at the Tamarack, when nothing seemed out of the ordinary.

We were all fairly excited by the noises and sensations we experienced inside the building, and were discussing everything that happened as we walked outside. Then to our surprise, just a few feet from the front of the building the K-2 meters lit up again. This had been an area where Barb had investigated before, but there previously had not been any EMF readings. For further confirmation, we set up the Tri-Field on a low brick wall and started to ask some questions.

What followed was a fascinating series of apparently direct responses from the meter's alarm—there were no sounds from the meter when we weren't asking questions, while some of our questions elicited an immediate response. It was all far beyond mere coincidence. In addition, Duane was able to measure a temperature difference around the meter, approximately ten degrees cooler than the ground and air just a couple of feet away. At several points, there were also distinct sounds coming from inside the building, sounds of someone walking on the broken glass in the hallway in front of us.

The story that emerged from our questions was unpleasant, to say the least, and it involved a man who was afraid. Before you have sympathy for this fearful spirit, however, consider the reason for his anxiety—he had taken advantage of a young girl and was afraid he would be caught.

The fear was palpable, but so was the feeling that there was more to this story. We all got the impression that this man made a habit of preying upon young girls, and wouldn't hesitate to use force. This was not a spirit you felt comfortable having behind you, and we soon discovered that we had all turned to face the building because we felt safer when we did. When four people instinctively react in the same way, it is a powerful moment!

The air around us then became even colder, and the K-2 meters spiked to red. Whatever it was felt very close, and at that moment

Mike tried to take my picture. The camera would not respond (the only time that happened all night), and he tried again and again.

"The camera will not focus on you," Mike announced.

"Oh, that makes me feel great," I replied.

The spot in front of the Westchester building
where we had the strange experiences.

As if I wasn't uncomfortable enough already, it would get even more intense. As I spoke those words, the meter's lights went red again. There was definitely someone or something else there, and too close for comfort for me. I stepped back a few feet, and fortunately the feeling subsided.

Now I know skeptics will say this experience was the result of our imaginations, and that there was some natural explanation for the reactions of the EMF meters. Before you draw such a conclusion, however, consider this: A couple of months after our investigation, Barbara uncovered some extraordinary information—in more recent years, a man who was illegally inhabiting one of the rooms in that building had sexually assaulted a young girl there!

Both the man and his victim are still alive, so their ghosts don't haunt the Tamarack, but perhaps the energy of the crime still lingers at that spot, adding to the energy of the same type of crimes committed there long ago. We have seen this at many other locations where a particular type of violent or abnormal behavior can be repeated through generations. Can negative patterns be imprinted on a place, which then influence those who come into contact with them? It certainly appeared to be the case here, and I felt a distinct sense of relief when we moved on to another building.

My relief was short-lived, however, as we next entered the Oxford House, which actually looked like an ordinary house, not a block of hotel rooms. This structure had been converted into guest rooms and had an odd layout of hallways and staircases, not making it immediately apparent how to get to a particular floor or location. In fact, we never found a way to get to the attic, except via a rusting fire escape which was far too dangerous to climb. Why would access inside the house be sealed off? Enquiring ghost investigators wanted to know, but they didn't want to risk their necks finding out!

Besides, there was plenty to occupy us in the rest of the house. As soon as we stepped inside, Mike reported that his heart had started racing. We also "heard" a woman screaming. I put it that way because it wasn't something that you could hear with your ears, but we all experienced it. This may not make sense, but if you have ever encountered such a phenomenon you know exactly what I mean. In any event, Mike seemed to be most affected by this place, so I suggested that he wait outside.

"Oh no, you can't stop me!" he replied.

"Okay, knock yourself out," I said, stepping aside and gesturing with a sweep of my arm, indicating that he should lead the way.

"Oh, thanks!" he said with a smile, and a hint of anxiety. "I didn't mean to go first."

I confess to some rather devilish laughter at that point which temporarily helped break the mood, which had been my objective. Although to be perfectly honest, Mike and I have been working together long enough that we occasionally have some fun by challenging one another to face our fears. It keeps us on our toes, and it keeps us going under often very stressful conditions.

We all had to be on our toes in that house, and not only from the forces we couldn't see. In one of the rooms we discovered that someone had been living there recently, as evidenced by empty food containers and beer bottles strewn all over the floor. It reminded us that a violent man had been living on the property several years earlier, and there were no guarantees that other unsavory characters weren't here now. (Which was another good reason to have a cop on your team!)

The aerial view of the Tamarack from the postcard:
A-theater, B-pool, C-Oxford House, D-Westchester building.

Throughout the house, Barbara continued sensing a very violent incident that had once taken place, and finally concluded that a woman had been strangled. That would certainly account for our initial experiences upon entering the house. This was probably the one building where we felt the most on edge, and those sensations would only intensify when we went into the basement.

Somewhere in the darkness of the large, musty, old basement, we clearly heard (with our ears this time!) men's voices. We couldn't make out any words as the voices were mumbling, but none of us had any doubt as to what we heard. There were also other sounds as if someone (or several someones) was moving around down there with us. And if all that wasn't unnerving enough, there was still the creepy feeling from the upstairs portion of the house, which seemed to seep down through the floorboards. Despite the noises and voices around us, we found ourselves constantly looking up, as if there was something threatening just over our heads...and perhaps there was.

We all took deep sighs of relief when we left the Oxford House. It was good to be out in the cool, clean air and walk off some of the accumulated negative energy. I believe it was at this point that I remarked that, "This place is alive with dead people, a literal ghost town." Typically, our investigations involve a single structure with one or two entities, so an enormous place like this was a real challenge to our physical, mental, and emotional stamina.

We kept on exploring a seemingly endless array of buildings and guest rooms. One of my favorite non-paranormal locations was a room that held one of those big chrome and stainless steel soda fountain and ice cream units. I am really into diners and drive-ins, and would love to have something like that in my home. I wanted to take a closer look at it, but it was on the second floor and many of the floorboards were rotted or completely missing. I could just imagine stepping in the wrong place and having both me and the soda fountain suddenly ending up on the first floor. Some things are better admired at a distance.

This warning is applicable for both the
physical and paranormal landscape here.

Our next stop was the indoor pool, where the spirits provided some of the best evidence of the night, although "best" may not exactly be the proper term. As we walked toward the expansive room with the high-ceiling, I had some trepidation that increased the closer we got. Barbara was just ahead of me, and right at the entrance she stopped abruptly as if she had come in contact with a physical object. She took a quick sharp breath, and put a hand over her stomach.

She explained that she had suddenly felt like someone had punched her in the stomach, knocking the wind out of her. Then her legs began stinging and more unpleasant sensations followed, with the overall feeling of getting "beaten up." As she spoke those words, there was a loud sound behind us, which could best be described like the "thud" of something, or someone, hitting the floor.

Again, not wanting anyone to push themselves too far, I suggested that Barbara not enter the pool area, but after catching her breath she wanted to go on. However, before taking another step she chastised the offending spirits and said that what had just occurred was "not nice" and to "please don't do it again." It's one thing to get the sense of a fight that had taken place, it's quite another to experience the physical impact. Unfortunately, that's one of the hazards of the job and we all know that doing what we do in places like this does set us up as potential targets, but it's all so fascinating it's worth the risk. (Of course, that's easy for me to say in this case, as I wasn't the one who got the paranormal punches.)

The deep end of the large pool had become something of a garbage dump and was filled with a huge pile of chairs and other unwanted items. Mike, Duane, and I gingerly poked around in the pile to see if there was anything interesting, and wouldn't you know I found a large plastic Halloween ghost. It was an historic moment, the first ghost I was physically able to capture on an investigation!

We quickly got serious again when we began hearing noises around the room. Then something pulled on Mike's leg. He described it as feeling like a little kid tugging on his pants' leg trying to get his attention, and it certainly did! I asked if there were any children present and there was an immediate soft knocking sound just to my left, followed by an even louder sound above our heads. With the acoustics in the large domed space, it was difficult to tell if the last sound had come from the ceiling itself, or if the sound was being reflected from somewhere below. In any event, these sounds were clearly not being made by any one of us!

The ghost I "captured" in the pool.

There continued to be soft sounds around the room, and Mike challenged the spirits to make a much louder noise. On cue, there came a loud banging sound that can clearly be heard on my digital recorder.

"That was noise!" I said, impressed by the quick and vigorous response to Mike's challenge.

"Come on, you can do better than that," Mike continued. "That was weak."

An instant later there was a very sharp and loud BANG!

"That was not weak," I said laughing, even more impressed by the definitive response.

The room then grew icy cold and Barbara began to see shadowy figures around us. The noises intensified and it certainly seemed like there were more than just children present. Were all these spirits the victims of accidental drownings in this pool, or did they congregate here now because this was a place where they once had so much fun?

It's all speculation, but the one thing that was certain was that we were not alone.

Mike in the deep end of the pool.

Eventually the activity subsided and we continued on to explore other areas. To our surprise, we found the door to the synagogue was wide open and the lights were on. We had passed by this room at least twice during the night, and the door had been shut. We called out to see if anyone was there, and searched the surrounding area. We found no one, and the next day Barbara spoke to the owner to confirm that he hadn't stopped by. But, could we rule out the possibility that someone was trespassing? Unfortunately, no. So, we couldn't get too excited by the open door and lights.

Next we went into the men's bathroom, which was a long, narrow room. The red lights lit up on Barbara's meter, and Mike suddenly had a "terrible headache." Barbara believed this was another area where there had been a serious fight, perhaps resulting in a fatality. Whatever had occurred had left enough of a residue that Mike felt too uncomfortable to stay.

The Men's Room where everyone felt uncomfortable.

We were all pretty much worn out by this point and decided to call it a night. As we packed up our gear, we talked about all the fascinating things that had happened. I was more than pleased and hoped that we had been able to get some photographic evidence in addition to the sounds that had been recorded. Little did I realize I was about to miss the best photo op of the night.

We carried all the bags of gear outside and while Mike loaded up his car, Barbara and Duane went back inside to turn off the lights and make sure everything was secure. It felt good to not be weighed down by all the cameras and meters I carry around during an investigation as I walked away a few yards to get a better view of the stars. Out of the corner of my eye, I saw some movement along the front of the building near the main lobby. There was enough moonlight that I was clearly able to see to see a figure in front of an outside door, which was about 125 feet away. The figure was all dark, so I couldn't tell who it was, but I assumed that it was Barbara or Duane locking up, even though I thought that door was already locked when we had checked it earlier.

I watched the figure for a few more moments, and started walking towards it. I was about to call out and see if Barb or Duane needed help with something, when I stopped dead in my tracks. Through a window to my right, I could see Barbara and Duane were still in the auditorium. I had a "does not compute" moment—you know, the "but if *they* are there, then *who* is that" type of moment. I turned quickly to check that Mike was still behind me, and then spun back around to see the dark figure still standing by the door.

My hands instinctively grabbed for my sides—like a gunslinger reaching for his six shooters—but my weapons of choice, my cameras, were all packed away. *Damn!* I then did the only thing I could do, which perhaps wasn't the most prudent thing. I broke into a run and headed straight for the dark figure. I started shouting "Hey, you!" and also called out for Mike. I didn't get very far before the figure vanished, and let me make that point very clear. The door did not open, so the figure did not go in the building, and the figure did not move away along the outside of the building, *it simply disappeared.*

I stopped running and just stood there and stared, hoping the figure would reappear. My heart was pounding, all my senses were on high alert, but I didn't see anything else. A few moments later Mike came running over to see what I was shouting about, and then Barbara and Duane joined us. I very excitedly explained what I had just witnessed, and we quickly all went over to the door where I had seen the mysterious figure.

There was a wooden platform in front of the door, and when I stepped onto it I discovered it was broken and rotted. My foot went through and I lost my balance, and only a very fast reaction by Duane to catch me kept me from falling. (Thanks, Duane!) The creaking, cracking wood made a lot of noise, and we realized there was no way a larger adult (the figure was definitely bigger than me) could have been silently standing on the unstable platform!

I was both extremely excited with the realization of what this was, and extremely disappointed that I was unable to get a photo or video of it. I can only console myself with the thought that it only appeared to me so clearly because it knew I would be unable capture its image. In any case, I was really pumped by the thrilling sighting and hoped that someday I would be able to return for another investigation before the place was demolished.

As of the publication of this book, some of the buildings have already been knocked down. Yet even if the entire place is leveled, no one can guarantee that this will release the myriad wandering spirits. And heaven help the occupants of any new structures that may be built on this property. To paraphrase the postcards, I have a feeling that these ghosts will never want to leave…

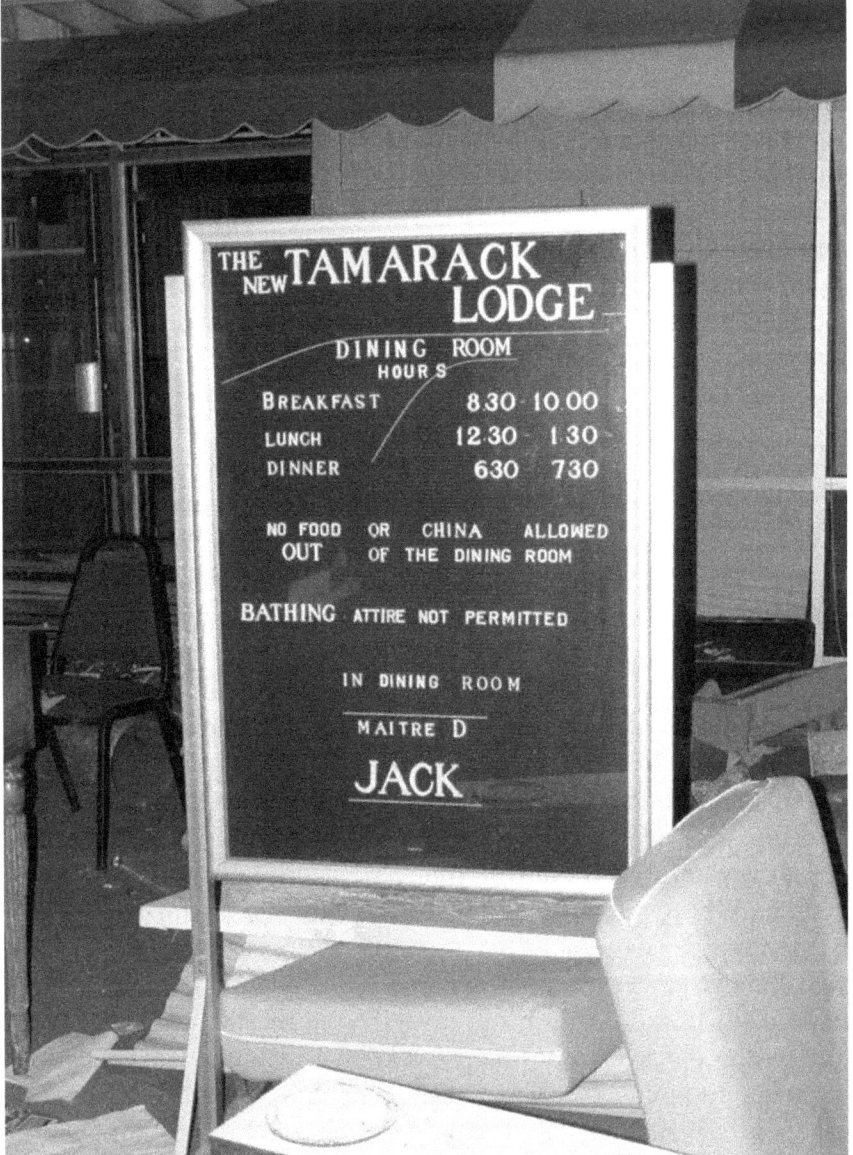

A reminder of the past which now stands in the pool area.

The former front desk area. A guest died on this spot
when he dropped dead at check-in.

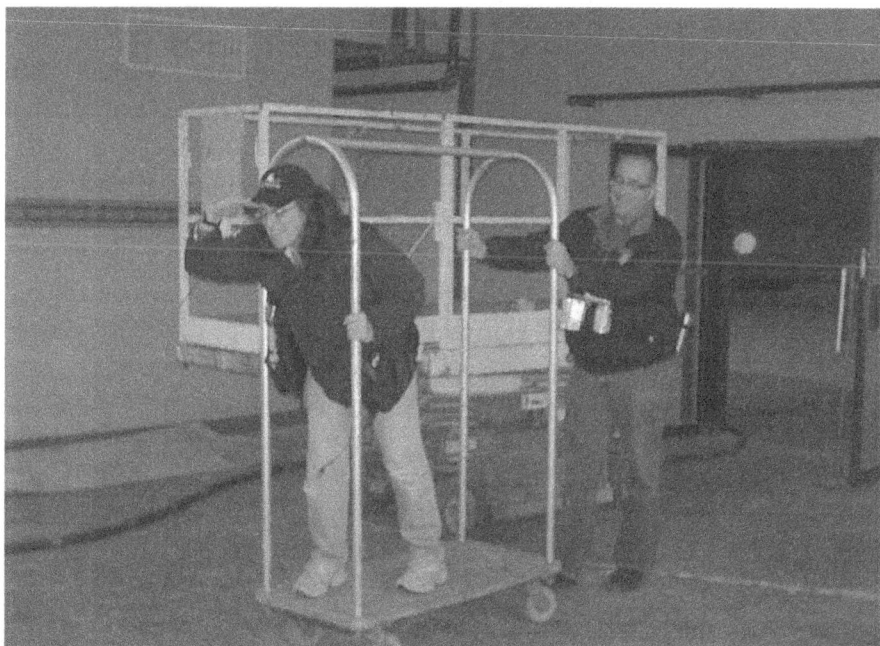

Barb took this photo of Mike and I with our new ghost hunting device.

Iron Island Museum
Buffalo, New York

Iron Island may sound like the name of some menacing location in a horror novel, but its origins are quite mundane. However, that doesn't mean it is without places that send chills up your spine...

It was the railroad that gave birth to Iron Island, and the area was so named as it is completely surrounded by railroad tracks. In the early 1900s, railroad employees settled here and the location became something of a self-sustaining island, or actually a city within a city. There were schools, stores, churches; everything a community needed lay within those iron rail boundaries. There may have been no other place like it, for here, no one grew up on the wrong side of tracks! (Or maybe everyone did!?)

The building at 998 Lovejoy Street, which now houses the Iron Island Preservation Society Museum, began as a Methodist-Episcopal church in 1885, and there was an addition built in 1898 for a Sunday school. Over the years, there must have been many weddings and christenings held here, as well as services for the dead—and the building was converted solely for that purpose in 1956 when it became a funeral home.

As Iron Island was a city within a city, this place became a building within a building, as the new owner put up walls and a ceiling inside which concealed the church's beautiful molding and stained glass windows. It's possible to still see these features by climbing a ladder through a small opening to the lofty attic space that was created by the construction of the funeral home ceiling. There is also a large basement with some odd, walled-in dirt areas. Needless to say, this all makes for a rather unique structure, which may in some ways contribute to the energies that move about the different levels—both physical and spiritual.

The funeral home changed hands a couple of times and continued to operate until the 1990s. It went out of business—not from a lack of people dying, but from some "stiff" competition (pun intended) from another nearby funeral parlor—and the owner decided to donate the building to the Iron Island Preservation Society, which was in need of a proper home for its museum and offices. The new museum opened in August of 2000

Curator Marge Thielman Hastreiter created displays of local history, including rooms specializing in the railroad and the military, and it's all presented in a wonderful informal setting that makes you feel like you are entering more of a home than a museum. And perhaps all of these artifacts have also brought a few more layers of energy to the building, as who can tell what—or who—is attached to old clothing and personal possessions?

When speaking of energy attached to objects, we must also consider that when the Society first occupied the building, they found 24 containers of human ashes in the basement. Even worse, years ago one container must have been knocked over as its grisly contents had spilled out all over the floor and no one had ever bothered to clean it up. Why had no one ever claimed the remains of all these poor souls? Were they all alone in the world, and are now seeking company in death?

Marge's daughter, Linda Hastreiter, is president of the organization, and she knew there was something unusual about the building right from the start. Her first unmistakable experience came during that first year. It was Christmas time, and chairs and tables had been set up for a party. Apparently, the party started early, as Linda heard chairs being moved, which were making quite a racket. The only problem was that she was alone.

Not even stopping to grab her car keys, she ran right out of the building. Fortunately, she had her cell phone with her and she called a friend for help, and admittedly used some rather colorful language to describe what had just happened. Linda then stood outside in a snowstorm waiting for her friend to come pick her up, and to this day, she won't go into the building alone.

Marge also has had many experiences, as she often spends long hours working on the collection. One sound she has heard on several occasions is her own name being spoken, even when no one else is in the building. Two visitors actually recorded one such instance—Marge was explaining to them about some of the strange things that happen, when she heard her name being called. She told the people that she just heard her name, and when the recording was played back, there it was!

In October of 2006, there was a freak snowstorm and power was out across the Buffalo area. Linda was away at the time, but her family sought refuge in the museum as it was one of the only places that had power and heat. They were all watching a Buffalo Bills football game on the TV in the back room, when Linda's brother saw a dark, shadowy figure walk down the hall and into the office, then walk out again. From his vantage point, it appeared as though the figure stopped and looked right at him! Marge saw the mysterious figure as well, but when they went to investigate, no one was there.

Many others have seen the Shadow Man, as he is now known, and there may be at least two photos of him. One picture was taken in the altar room, and reflected in the mirror is a dark figure of a man. Another picture was taken on January 15, 2009, the day an American Airlines jet made the spectacular emergency landing in the Hudson River. The photo was shot looking into the back room where news of the plane crash was on the TV. No one was in the room, and the photo is clear enough to see the image of the jet in the water, and next to the TV is standing what looks like a man all in black! Was he watching out of concern for the crew and passengers, or just wondering if he was about the get a lot more company on the other side?

In August of 2007, Linda—who previously hadn't been a believer in the paranormal—realized it was time to start collecting evidence and documenting all the strange occurrences. Local paranormal investigator Greg Hoffman assembled a team and got to work, and it wasn't long before things started to happen. The following are some of the highlights from Greg's team, museum staff, and visitors:

> Linda and Greg were trying to get EVPs one night, and they did get a clear child's voice saying "boat." They weren't sure what that meant, but later several psychics claimed that there was the spirit of a 6 or 7-year-old boy named Tommy in the room. In fact, while searching the records of the funeral home, Linda did find that in 1966, there was a 6-year-old boy named Tommy who died of leukemia and was waked in that room. Was it just a coincidence? Perhaps, but consider this: A relative of Tommy's visited the museum, and said that the boy's favorite thing had been to go fishing out on the lake in his father's boat.

> The building is equipped throughout with infrared surveillance cameras that Linda can monitor at home on her computer. Late one night after closing, she was at home watching in amazement as one of the lamps in the military room kept turning itself on and off. There were also what appeared to be white balls of light shooting across the room. (During our investigation, Mike tested the switch on the lamp. It wasn't at all loose, and was actually kind of hard to turn, so it couldn't possibly have been switching on and off by itself.)

> A man and his 12-year-old daughter were visiting the museum. At one point the girl, who was looking quite shaken, came up to her father and Linda. When asked what happened she was reluctant to say, as she didn't think anyone would believe her. When pressed she relented, and said that she had been alone in the military room, kneeling down to look at the large, framed set of photos of the local people who served in WWII. Suddenly, she felt a breath in her ear and a hand on her shoulder. Terrified, she jumped up and ran. Later, when Linda examined the surveillance video, she saw the girl kneeling down in front of the photos. Then, for no visible reason, she jumped to her feet in a panic and ran out of the room. The girl didn't know she was being taped, so there wouldn't have been any reason to put on an act.

The Military Room. The large frame leaning against the wall to the right contains photos of local residents who served in WWII.

> In the altar room (the altar is not original to this church), people claim to see the pages of the Bible move. The funeral home used this room as a coffin showroom, and two of the kneelers, where mourners would kneel to pray next to the coffin, are in the room. The photo of the Shadow Man was taken here.

> The Terminal Room is not named because people succumbed here to fatal diseases, it's because of the large train terminal model. There's a small opening in the ceiling and a tall ladder, so people can take a peek at the former church ceiling, woodwork, and stained glass. Several visitors (with no prior knowledge) claimed that when they poked their heads up through the hole, something would growl in their ear and blow their hair. One skeptic who had heard about this laughed about it, until he tried it himself. A second after he climbed the ladder he hurried back down looking very scared. He said that something growled right in his ear.

The Terminal Room. People climbing this ladder and sticking their heads through the hole in the ceiling have been growled at.

> Footsteps are often heard in the attic, but until recently there was only insulation and no boards to walk on.

> Linda recorded an EVP of someone calling her name, which was slow and whispered, like" Linnn...daaahh..."

➤ Five different psychics on five separate occasions claimed that many bodies of children are buried in the dirt behind one of the stone walls. Was the church constructed on top of a children's cemetery, or was there something more sinister involved?

➤ Several psychics reported seeing a teenaged girl on the floor of the basement. She was tied up with tape over her mouth.

➤ During an investigation in the basement, the air suddenly grew colder, the K2 meter lit up, and witnesses saw a short, dark figure peer out from behind the furnace, then suddenly pull back and disappear.

Are there bodies of children buried in this basement?

When Linda finished relaying this amazing paranormal laundry list of phenomena to me and Mike during our visit, I said in my best mock-disappointment tone, "Is that all?" Clearly, this was one very active location, and we couldn't wait to get started on our own investigation.

Our chance came a few months after Greg contacted me to tell me about the Iron Island Museum. He had been an investigator at the Rolling Hills Asylum and had read my book containing the account of our adventures there, and thought the museum was our kind of place. He was right.

It was a gray and rainy Wednesday in April of 2009 when Mike and I hit the road. And for those of you who have read past books, do I even need to say that I had baked some dark chocolate brownies for the trip? There are only two essentials for one of our road trips—gasoline and brownies, and not necessarily in that order.

When we reached Buffalo, our first stop was the *U.S.S. The Sullivans* destroyer at the Naval and Military Park (which also has a cruiser and a submarine). The ship is allegedly haunted, and while we did not conduct an actual investigation, Mike did have his K2 meter and found some high readings by the door to the bridge. Perhaps this was from some natural source, but without knowing what the electrical system was like in the surrounding areas we couldn't say for sure.

The only thing I can state with any certainty is that Mike and I ran around the ships like a couple of little kids. We shamelessly and gleefully turned every lever, pushed every button, and "fired" every gun. However, it was not all fun and games, as we did read about the heroic battles, the long voyages at sea, the hardships of the crew, and of course, about the five Sullivan brothers for whom the ship is named, who all died during WWII. It was because of their tragedy that the Navy stopped putting brothers on the same ship.

After a long day of travel, our strenuous military exercise, and with a long night of ghost hunting before us, we naturally needed some sustenance. We didn't need anything much, just simple, wholesome food—Yeah, right! We made a beeline to the Seneca Casino Thunder Falls Buffet, and I am forced to censor the details of the ensuing culinary onslaught, as the amount of food we consumed would unduly frighten the reader. Now, back to the ghosts…

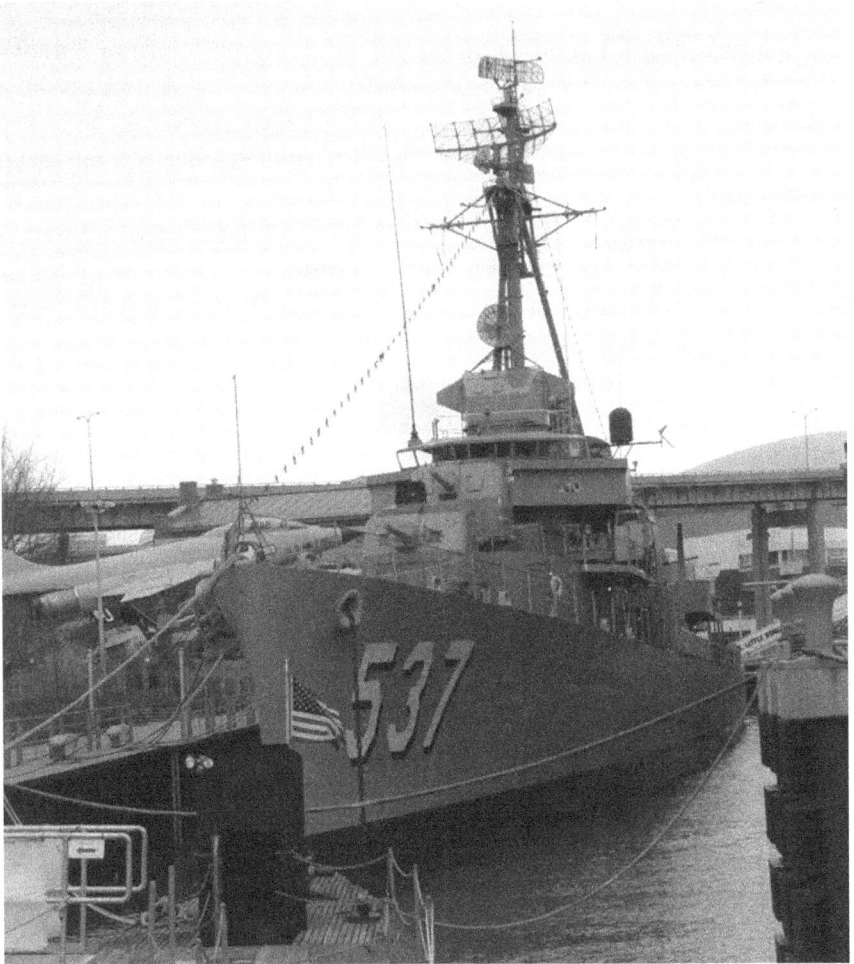

U.S.S. The Sullivans

Joining us that night at the Iron Island Museum was Linda, Greg, his son, Scott, and Jennifer Glowszak. We began with Linda giving us a tour of the building from top to bottom. She also let us listen to some of the fascinating EVPs and look at the photographic evidence they've collected. There was a lot going on within the many walls of this building, and there was an attic, a basement, and three main rooms to cover. Mike and I talked it over and decided how we were going to approach the investigation, and where to set up all the equipment.

Things got off to a quick start when one of Mike's motion detectors went off. The piercing alarm startled us all, but even more so when we realized it couldn't have been a living person that set it off. Mike had put the detector by the front door, aimed across the hall. Someone would have had to come through the front doorway to trigger it, and Mike was in the middle room and the rest of us were in various locations in the back of the building. Just as the alarm was going off, Greg noticed that the motion-activated lights in the parking area came on. Had something simultaneously tripped the lights and the motion detector? We definitely got he sense that it was "game on" from this point.

Mike's motion detector went off in this hallway near the front door. The Shadow Man has been seen in this hall.

We decided to start in the front room and work our way back. We were all sitting in the dark with K2 meters and digital recorders, with a camcorder aimed into the middle room (there is a wide opening between rooms). Shortly after beginning, we noticed the recording light on the camcorder had gone off. Mike checked it out and found that the freshly-charged battery was now completely drained—several hours of power were gone in just minutes. There would be a total of five fully-charged batteries that would fail that night, some before we even had a chance to use them!

I was asking some questions, looking and listening intently for a response, and got one when I asked, "How many are here?" There was a sound from the back of the building near the office, as if something was moving. We all heard it.

A minute or so later I started "hearing" the name Brandy over and over again. No one knew of anyone connected to the place with that name. I asked if anyone named Brandy was with us, and one of the K2 meters flashed a couple of lights. Not a resounding yes, but it did appear to be a direct response. Later on that night in the altar room, I once again kept sensing the name Brandy, as being short for Brandon. Perhaps further research of the burial records or history of the former church will determine if there was such a person here at one time—either living or dead.

I then asked if whoever was with us could come over to our meters, and immediately both Mike's and mine had a few lights flicker. Then I asked if it was a man and my meter's light glowed bright and steady for several seconds.

"I'll take that as a yes," I said, pleased that we seemed to have someone willing and able to communicate.

"Was your funeral held here?"

Again the lights glowed strong. It's very creepy now that I think about what I had just asked, but at the time it was just exciting.

I started running through the decades to try to pinpoint when this man had died, but there was nothing. Then I realized I had started with the 1950s when the place became a funeral home, but the old church must have held many services for its deceased congregation members. I then asked if this man's funeral had taken place before it was a funeral home, back in the time when it was a church. The meter's lights suddenly glowed the brightest so far, as an icy cold air mass engulfed me.

"Wow, that was strong!" Linda commented, as we all agreed it was an unequivocal affirmative. We were apparently dealing with a spirit from at least a generation or two earlier.

We tried a few other questions with no success, until I asked if this man was looking for someone. When Linda played back that section on her digital recorder, we all heard a voice say, "No!" A few minutes later, I asked if the man needed help, and again, the word "No" was recorded. We got the sense that he was quite set in his ways and was not happy about us poking our noses in his business.

We all moved to the middle room where all the military items were displayed. A few minutes later (at 10:15pm to be exact) even though all the lights were out everything seemed to get darker. How could that be possible? We all noticed it, and fortunately Linda believed she knew why. There's a doctor's office next door and he has an outdoor light, just bright enough to illuminate the interior of the museum ever so slightly. The next day Linda checked the surveillance cameras, and sure enough, at 10:15pm the doctor's outdoor light shut off. A good piece of detective work on Linda's part, which prevented us from erroneously concluding some sinister force of darkness was at play!

If I may digress for a moment, this illustrates a lesson I have learned over my years of ghost hunting—make sure you make time checks frequently. You don't all have to synchronize your watches and be compulsive about it, but if I hadn't said the darkening occurred at 10:15pm, Linda would have had a lot of surveillance tape to go through. Also, as we often have multiple cameras and recorders going, if you keep mentioning the time you can easily check to see which ones captured a particular sound or event, which can also help triangulate where a sound originated. For me in particular, since I need to reconstruct investigations as accurately as possible for my books, my trusty Luminox watch is an absolutely essential piece of ghost hunting equipment.

Anyway, back to sitting in the funeral home chairs waiting for signs from the dead.

After a few minutes, Mike decided to put out a bit of a challenge to the spirits in a stern, but not threatening, tone. He stated that we had driven many hours to get here, and that the spirits could do better than produce a few EVPs and EMF readings. He explained that we weren't there to harm anyone or send them away, we just wanted to talk. In fact, Mike sounded very much like a father admonishing his children to put forth their best effort.

Suddenly, I thought I detected movement in the corner of the room near the hall. I looked more closely, and sure enough, there appeared to be a short figure that was cautiously sticking his head out. I gave it another couple of seconds to make sure of what I was seeing, then said that I was looking at a short figure moving in the corner.

"Was it like he was peeking?" Jennifer asked. "Like the figure of a child?"

That was exactly what it looked like, a shy child peeking around the corner to see what we were up to. Jennifer explained that's what other people have seen, and they believe it may be Tommy—or at least that's the name to which he seems to respond. Everyone turned to look in that corner, and everyone either detected some movement or saw the small, shadowy figure. It also became so cold I started to shiver.

Mike's stern, fatherly recriminations instantly transitioned to compassionate, fatherly encouragement. He softly told the boy not to be scared, and that he could come over to us if he wanted to. The temperature seemed to drop another ten degrees and we could hear someone moving closer.

"I have this really cool thing here with lights that change colors," Mike said, holding his K2 off to his left. "Show me that you can make the lights light up. Show me you can do it...Look! Look! Three lights! Oh my God!"

As if on cue, Mike's K2 meter now had three lights on. But that was nothing compared to what was about to happen. I suddenly felt a great sadness and loneliness. I was just about to ask if the little boy was lonely when Mike spoke.

"I'm incredibly sad right now," he said, clearly overcome with emotion. "My hand is ice cold."

"Can you make it go up to orange?" Jennifer asked. "I know you can do it, you've done it before."

Orange! Again, in an immediate response the K2 meter now had four lights on, the fourth of which is orange. We were amazed.

"That was awesome, you did it!" Mike said.

We continued with some other questions and continued to hear sounds—in fact, there were sounds all around us in the room. The meter again lit up when Mike asked if the boy liked trains, Jean recorded a sound that appeared to be a child giggling, and Linda heard tapping.

This sad little boy projected a strong presence and we all felt it. I knew Mike was the most affected, but I didn't know until later that he had actually felt the child take hold of his hand, the hand that held the K2 meter! The contact allowed him to directly experience this boy's loneliness and Mike freely admitted it brought tears to his eyes. This deep connection would literally haunt him for many days, and Mike still feels bad about the plight of this poor little soul.

As we all sat in the darkness with this gentle spirit, there was a sudden shift in the atmosphere. The sounds stopped and the K2 meter went back to its single "on" indicator light. We needed a break—especially Mike—so we took a few minutes and went back to where we had all of our gear. I had a spiral-bound book of index cards I was using to take notes and Mike went right over to it and started writing quickly. He wanted to get his thoughts and feelings on paper while the experience was still fresh.

As I write this now about a month later, I have that index card in front of me. I can still picture the emotion in Mike's face, which reflected in the words he wrote: "Very sad, very overwhelming," and then "TOUCHING MY HAND" underlined twice with emphasis. I've said this many times in the past, but it's worth repeating for those who think ghost hunting is all fun and games— this is serious work and can be very upsetting when an emotional encounter like this takes place.

We did not speak about this at the time, but Mike also wrote, "Male presence, angry, made child leave—told him he should know better...child hiding in corner—watching, wants to play but can't...<u>SORRY</u>."

When we all took our places in that room again a few minutes later, I think we all sensed that it was a different presence that now held sway over the room. Instead of speaking kindly to a lonely child, we all seemed to take on a confrontational tone. Then Linda asked if the man from upstairs had frightened the boy away. The K2 shot up and I let out a short gasp in surprise at both Linda's question and the meter's reaction. A man scaring away the child—that was exactly what Mike had written down!

Mike's protective nature, especially toward kids, immediately came to the forefront.

"Picking on some poor lost kid, must make you feel like a real tough guy," he said with genuine anger.

"Do we make you angry?" Linda asked, and the K2 lights blinked on as a confirmation. "Good!"

Linda was not simply pleased that there was a reaction, but that the adult male spirit was apparently displeased by our presence.

Throughout this exchange with what was generally perceived to be a mean, bullying spirit that frightens children for fun, I was sensing something a little different. To be sure, I did not like this man, but I didn't picture him as someone who thought he was doing anything wrong. If I had to write a profile of him, I would place him back at least a hundred years. He was a strict clergyman who firmly believed that children should be seen and not heard—to the point where what we would consider very harsh discipline, if not outright abuse, this man considered to be good for the soul. And, he saw no reason to let a little thing like death keep him from trying to impose his iron will on defenseless children.

We obtained some similar results in the altar room, then moved on to the basement where we all continued to ask questions and look for responses on the meters. When asked if there was more than one spirit in the basement, we had an immediate and strong response. There was definitely a feeling that a lot of negative things had

The Altar Room. The two kneelers were used in the funeral home and would have been placed next to the casket.

transpired down there, things that had left an unpleasant psychic imprint. It also felt as if there were quite a variety of active entities milling about for various reasons.

Unfortunately, the musty basement air was getting to me and I started coughing—which is not conducive to any attempt at gathering evidence. I tried to hold it back, but my sinuses and throat were clearly not happy, so I reluctantly went upstairs for some water and to take a break. The very long day was also taking a toll, and there's no sense trying to conduct an investigation if you aren't sharp mentally.

Mike and I did crawl through to the attic and spent some time there, but either nothing else was happening or we were just too tired to notice! If we didn't have to get up early to drive home the next day we might have tried to stick it out a little longer, but as it was, we would probably only be getting a few hours sleep once we got back to the hotel and took some time to unwind. I don't know about other ghost hunters, but I am rarely able to quickly shift from high speed to neutral after an investigation, especially when so many amazing things have just taken place.

On the long drive home the next morning, I could see that Mike was still troubled by the lonely, frightened spirit of the little boy. He felt that there should have been something he could have done to help this lost soul, but perhaps in that moment of contact some good did come out of it. I always say that compassion is never wasted, so I would like to think the boy found some comfort from Mike's compassionate and supportive energies.

As for the many other spirits of the Iron Island Museum, time will tell if further research reveals any more of their hidden secrets. And perhaps some digging in the basement may reveal something even more solid?

If you are fortunate enough to be able to visit the beautiful Niagara Falls/Buffalo area, in addition to the usual sightseeing spots, do try to make the time to go to this museum in the former church/funeral home. You will learn a lot about the people and history of the area, and you may also be lucky enough to experience something on another level. Of course, there are no iron-clad guarantees that a ghost will cross your path, but your chances of a paranormal encounter at the Iron Island Museum may be worth the trip. And if you are brave enough to spend the night in this very haunted building, group ghost hunts are available.

Just remember that it may not all be fun and games, and in the darkness of the night a lost little boy may slip his icy hand in yours, and you may never be the same again...

For more information go to:
http://www.ironislandmuseum.com/

The Iron Island Museum
998 Lovejoy Street
Buffalo, New York 14206
716-892-3084

The Latest Update:

Before going to press, I checked with Linda and Greg for the latest activity. Linda reported that she just recently "saw the Shadow Man in the central terminal room" and "a little shadow of a kid running down the hallway."

Greg wrote the following:

"It's been pretty active since you were here. 'Tommy' has been especially friendly, and has been caught on quite a few evp's. In one he has actually said his name, which as you know is very rare for an evp. I was instructing a group of inexperienced individuals on gathering evp's. We were in the middle room (Military), and I was showing them how to start the session by including the time, date, location and area and also vocalizing our names for voice recognition. After we finished with our names we started the session and after a period of time we took a break. They were reviewing their recordings, and after giving our names for the voice recognition, we had one extra voice saying 'Tommy' clear as day! It was like he was playing a game with us."

As I said before, it's worth the trip to Iron Island!

And a few more scenes from the Naval Park…

Mike making the world safe for democracy.

That's me scanning the skies over Buffalo for Kamikazes.

Oh no, Mike, don't press *that* button!

Toll at the Train Station
Middletown, NY

All photos in this story are courtesy of Michael Worden,
unless otherwise noted.

Apparently, Chip Lewis can't get enough of the dead, but perhaps I had better explain that. He is the caretaker of the Walkill Cemetery and lives in the very haunted house on the cemetery grounds that I wrote about in *Ghost Investigator Volume 7*. One would think Chip would have had his fill of dealing with restless spirits, but such is not the case—his experiences have led him to ghost hunting with Mechanicstown Paranormal Research, and they've found the ideal location to investigate not far from home.

For those who lived in Orange County in the 1980s or 90s, chances are you dined at the Rusty Nail in Middletown, or at least know of the name from the billboard on Route 17 that still stands to this day. The popular restaurant had a great setting in the old

Mechanicstown train station from the O&W Railroad. The station was closed in 1924, and the building was divided down the middle and became a two-family dwelling before being turned into a restaurant.

In the 1970s, Chip's sister lived in the converted station, and family members quickly became aware of strange things going on. Chip admitted he would baby-sit for his sister's children, but would leave as soon as she got home, refusing to ever spend the night there. Chip's friends felt the same way about the spooky old building. Given the opportunity to spend the night, they would instead sleep out in the adjacent woods.

Inexplicable footsteps and other sounds were always heard throughout the house. One night his nephew came running out of the bathroom in a panic, as he swore a dark, shadowy figure had walked in. On many occasions, an older man with a beard was spotted both inside and outside of the building, with passersby often asking who the man was standing by a second floor window. This bearded apparition looked so real and solid that one night a friend asked Herbie, one of the residents, if his father was visiting.

"My father is in Florida," Herbie replied, puzzled as to why his friend would ask him such a question.

"Then who is that old guy with the beard sitting on the stairs?" his friend countered.

Unfortunately, when he turned to point to the old man who had been sitting just a few yards away, no one was there.

Clues to the identity of this bearded man may lie in a photograph Chip discovered during his research. It's a picture of the train station around the turn of the century with the station master standing on a loading dock—and he looks remarkably like the eyewitness accounts of the apparition. The station master and his family did live in the building for many years and he was responsible for keeping everything in order. Perhaps he has taken his responsibilities to the grave and remains to keep an eye on the place?

There may also be evidence as to the identity of another spirit in the old train station. One night during an investigation, Chip was on the first floor and his fellow investigators, Justin Hermen and Bob Dunham, were on the third floor. The two men called down to Chip and asked where the music was coming from. Chip hadn't heard any music, but the men insisted someone was playing a guitar in the building. They all checked inside and out, but never found the source of the mysterious music.

However, there is a possible explanation. Herbie was a guitar player in a band, and in the 1980s he was on his way home to the train station. At the intersection just a few hundred yards away, his motorcycle was struck by a car and he was killed. Chip vividly recollects the night of the tragic accident, because he was actually on the fire truck called to the scene!

The former loading platform on the right, where the bearded man has been seen. He has also appeared on the second floor balcony.

The chef of the Rusty Nail and other employees used to complain about all the noise on the second floor and wondered who was always walking around up there. Slight problem here: For some reason, the restaurant owner had removed the two staircases to the second floor, so no one could have been up there!

I always wonder about the motives behind such a drastic move as tearing out two large staircases that removed all access to two expansive floors of work, living, or storage space. (Can you *ever* have enough storage space?) Were the old staircases and upper floors simply deemed unsafe, or did the unceasing footsteps prompt him to try to keep whatever was walking around upstairs from coming down to the main floor?

Over the years there has been a lot of other activity in the old train station, including:

- During one of their investigations, Chip had a camcorder aimed at the open door to the balcony on the second floor. While reviewing the tape, they were stunned to see a dark figure move across the room and out onto the balcony, then poke its head back through the doorway as if realizing it was visible.

- They have obtained several EVPs of a woman's voice.

- Chip and Mark Markle had stopped by and were checking the outside of the building to make sure it was secure (people have often tried to break in). Chip noticed that someone had posted a flyer on the building, so he stood there and read it to Mark, who he thought he could see out of the corner of his eye was standing just a few feet away. When Mark didn't respond, Chip turned and found that he was nowhere in sight. So who had been standing next to him?

When Mike and I found out we had a chance to investigate another train station, we couldn't wait. Of course if we had any sense, we would never step foot in another train station after getting locked in the last one by an evil presence (*Ghost Investigator Volume 7*). But you have to be at least a little bit crazy to do what we do, so we were anxious to get into the old O&W Railroad building.

When we arrived the following group was all ready to begin: Chip Lewis, Bob Delham, Dennis and Becky Baudentistel, Dominick and Nicole Guardino, Mark Markle, and Brenda Ferranta. We decided to break up into two groups, and Bob and Dominick would go upstairs with Mike and I, while the others would head into the basement. Most importantly, Dominick would be carrying the thermal imaging camera, an extremely cool piece of equipment that admittedly made Mike and I jealous.

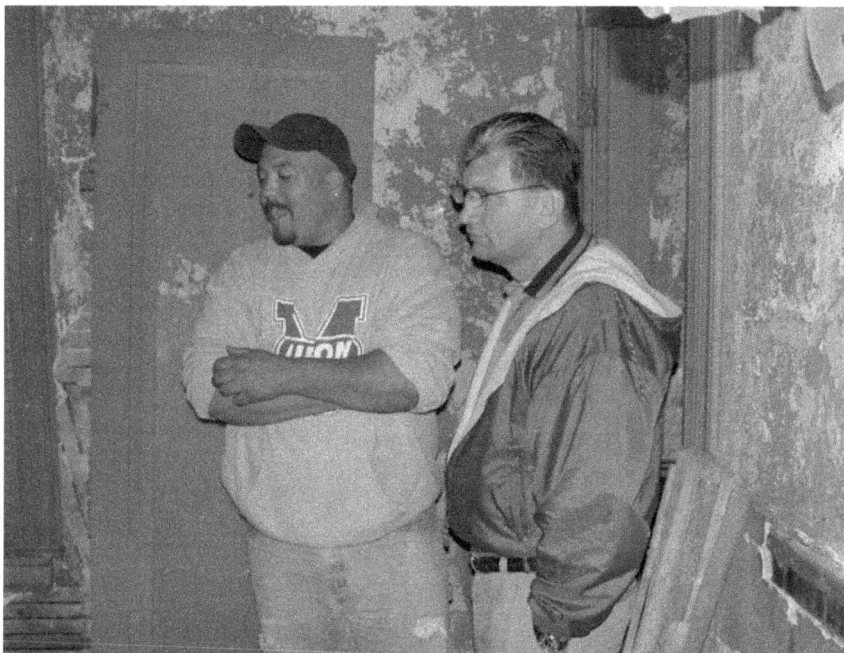

Bob Delham and Mark Markle against
the backdrop of the deteriorating interior.

As I previously mentioned, both staircases to the second floor had been torn out, so the only access was from a ladder they had brought. It was placed in a small opening in the ceiling and it was a bit of a tight fit for the men, but awkward to navigate for everyone, especially while carrying a lot of sensitive and expensive cameras and equipment. I secured everything in the zippered pockets of my SWAT vest, climbed the ladder, and crawled out onto the second floor.

Dominick had already come up, Mike was on the ladder halfway through the opening, and Bob was waiting behind him. I leaned over to take Mike's camera so it didn't get damaged as he maneuvered his way through the hole, and as I straightened up I saw a pair of legs in dark pants go from left to right across a small landing at the top of an adjacent staircase to the third floor. As I

The small opening to the second floor which
is underneath a staircase to the third floor.

thought it would only be the four of us up here I was concerned that
others would be moving around and any sounds we heard would
have to be discounted if we didn't know exactly who was where at
all times.

"Who else is up here?" I asked Dominick.

"I was the first one up here," he replied.

No, I thought. *Clearly he is mistaken.*

"I just saw someone come down onto the landing up there and
go off to the right," I said, as certain of what I saw as he was in
continuing to insist that he was the first up the ladder, and there
wasn't any other way to get up here.

If that was true...

No way! I thought. *Things can't be happening already!*

I grabbed my flashlight and bolted up the staircase. There was a
solitary room off to the right of the small landing and it was empty.
Calling out to see if anyone was on the second or third floors, I spun
around and ran in the other direction, thinking perhaps that whoever
it was had gone back the way he had come. I rushed from room to

110

room, checking every nook and cranny, but there was no sign of anyone. I was both thrilled and annoyed.

I just witnessed what appeared to be a solid pair of legs walk past and we didn't even have time to set up any cameras or equipment yet. I always preach that you should go into a haunted location ready to go, but I didn't think I would already see something about three seconds into the investigation!

I came back down to the second floor and Mike asked what was going on, clearly wondering why I was already running around like a crazy person. I explained what I saw, and fortunately Bob was able to confirm that he heard footsteps above his head on that landing while he was on the ladder directly below. So the game was afoot, literally, and I hoped whoever it had been would not be playing cat and mouse games and messing with us all night. Wishful thinking, as I was about to be messed with, big time.

We went up to the third floor and checked everything with our EMF meters, but didn't get even the slightest reading—until Dominick mentioned Herbie's name. Suddenly my meter had two of the four lights light up. It was brief, but definitely a reaction, and timed as if it was a direct response to the mentioning of the name of the former resident who had died in the street from a tragic accident.

Several minutes later I started hearing the word "toll" and picturing someone having to give someone else a coin. I asked if anyone knew if any toll roads used to be in the area, assuming this had something to do with the history of the place. No one could think of any toll roads in the vicinity, but that was not the end of it. One of those persistent little voices in my head kept repeating, "Pay the toll. You have to pay the toll."

I tried to ignore it for a while, which became easy at one point when Bob heard footsteps behind him up a short staircase. Through the thermal imager Dominick saw a round shape low to the floor move behind Bob. The shape did not give off a high heat signature of an animal or person, but instead appeared relatively cool. We all hurried up the several stairs to the spot, but couldn't find anything.

I checked the area with my EMF meter and while nothing registered on the instrument, my hand started to tingle. I described it being like feeling static electricity and Mike bent down and also felt the tingly sensation near the floor. Dominick said the area around our hands looked hotter through the thermal camera than the

I'm standing on the spot where I first saw the legs, which
walked off to the right. From the position where Mike took this
photo you can see all of me, but when I witnessed the figure I was
a few steps over to the right, so my view was limited to the waist down.

surrounding area, and we could not explain either the heat or the
static feel.

Due to the size of the image Dominick saw, and the somewhat
mischievous feel to the activity, I asked if anyone had ever
witnessed any signs that the spirits of children were roaming about
the old train station, but they weren't aware of any reports. Then we

heard more footsteps, always in places where we weren't, and the chase continued for a while.

Mike's flash photo in the darkness catches me lost in thought as I continue to "hear" something about paying a toll. This was the area where Dominick saw the image in the thermal camera and we felt the static electricity,

Once the flurry of activity quieted down a bit, the word "toll" resurfaced and I once again asked if there could be some connection. I explained that I don't claim to a psychic per se, but that there had been some interesting occurrences on recent investigations.

"Yeah, she's been on a roll," Mike confirmed.

The image of paying some sort of toll just wouldn't go away and at the risk of appealing foolish I said, "This may be one of the stupidest things I've ever done, but does anyone have a quarter?"

I thought for a moment that if this was just something symbolic, that any coin should do, but I did specifically ask first for a quarter. Bob had one and gave it to me. I held it up an announced that I was paying the requested toll, and then tossed it into a room. I then suggested that we split up and go to the four sides of the third floor and try to see if at least one of us could finally be in the same room as the shifting activity.

"Hey, I found a quarter on the floor," Mike joked as he entered the room where I just tossed the coin. Laughter always helps to break the tension on an investigation.

"Okay, you kept getting into my head," I said out loud, as I settled into a crouching position on the floor of an adjacent room. "I paid the toll and now I need a clear sign or I'm going to take back that quarter."

Immediately I "heard" a name. I whispered into my digital recorder, "Possibly the name Simon."

The instant I said the name something knocked loudly on the window sill right behind me, then a series of taps continued along the length of the sill.

"Oh, jeez!" I yelled, jumping to my feet and spinning around. An icy chill swept over me and I admit to being startled by the loud sound—which fortunately *was* captured on my digital recorder.

Everyone hurried into the room and I explained what had happened. There weren't any tree limbs that could have hit the building near the window, no loose boards or trim, and anyway, the sound was clearly *inside* the room with me.

As I was knocking on the window sill to demonstrate what I had heard, Dominick said he just heard something behind him. We all stood quietly for a few moments and then there were some loud noises on the second floor right below us. The tension was broken—it had to have been someone from the other group moving chairs or a table…or so we thought at first.

Dominick called down the stairs and asked who it was. There was no response. We all exchanged quick glances, as the tension level ratcheted up again. He called out loud again. Silence. There are several holes in the floor and we looked all around to see who had moved the furniture "as gracefully as a bull in a china shop," as Dominick so aptly described it. There was no one. We later confirmed that no one from the other group had come upstairs. It must have taken a lot of energy to make such a loud sound. I was impressed.

We continued our systematic investigation, and eventually came upon a room on the second floor that can only be reached by climbing over or under very large metal ducts. There had been reports that someone's camera would not work in that room, so I crawled under one dusty duct along the dirty floor and over another to get to the room to try for myself. My camera worked fine, but something else odd happened.

I was standing in the center of the room facing a wall about eight feet away. It was fairly dark, with just the faintest of light in which I could see the room's features. After a few minutes, I noticed a short shadow directly in front of me, under the window. As the others were in the room behind me, I assumed they had some sort of light that was casting a shadow, my shadow—until it moved quickly to my left and almost doubled in height!

I took a step back as I was naturally a bit surprised, but still suspected it was my own shadow, and that whoever held the light source in the other room had simply shifted quickly over to my right. Not taking my eyes off the shadow—which seemed oddly three-dimensional—I asked what lights everyone was using and who was behind me to my right. They all replied that they were using infrared, which the human eye can't see and therefore can't create a visible shadow, and that they were all standing to my left!

I turned quickly to confirm that, as I was acutely aware that if it wasn't my shadow, I was alone in the room with something I would really rather not be alone in a room with! When I saw that the three men were indeed off to my left and no one was using visible light, the hairs stood up on the back of my neck. I took a deep breath and turned back to face my shady new friend, but he had gone—or at least the visible part of him was gone.

I heard three heavy, wheezing, rasping breaths, and they seemed to be originating quite close to me in the dark room. But you never know how sound travels, so just to be sure I asked the somewhat awkward question, "Are any of you breathing heavy out there?" I'm not sure if I was relieved or distressed to find out it wasn't one of the three men!

Since activity was clearly hopping in this room, Mike decided to crawl under the ducts to join me, which was considerably more difficult for him given the difference in our sizes. Upon entering the room, he immediately felt uncomfortable, which was the first time all night he encountered such unpleasant sensations. We were both

An infrared photo of me in the room where I saw a shadow on the wall to my left. The large air duct is in front of the doorway.

Later in the evening, I explain how the shadow grew in height.

on edge, and found that we both kept looking over to the same side of the room as if we expected to see someone standing there.

We measured the approximate height of the larger shadow I saw, and it was about five foot six inches. We scanned the room for EMF, but found nothing. We waited patiently for some time for any more visual or audio evidence, but other than the skin-crawling sensation that we were not alone, nothing further occurred. Of course, given the amazing things I had just seen and heard, I can't say that I was the least bit disappointed.

At this point we decided to take a break and compare notes with the other group. We met on the main floor by the bar and out of the blue I heard Chip say something about a quarter. I wondered how he could have possibly already found out about the quarter I threw, as we had all just come down the ladder. He again repeated something about a quarter and everyone in his group was laughing. I was very confused and asked what he was talking about.

"I lost a quarter here tonight," Chip replied, much to my surprise. He went on to explain that Mark had found a piece of paper in the basement that contained some typical bar room humor where you asked someone for a quarter, which bought them membership in a club—the likes of which contained some rather crude language that I will not repeat here, but I'm sure you get the idea.

Mark had asked Chip for a quarter, which he gave him, and then Mark gave him the membership "certificate." So in essence, Chip had paid his "toll" with a quarter.

"No way!" I said in amazement. "You honestly took a quarter? Seriously?"

What were the chances that someone in both groups, isolated from one another, would ask another member of the group for a quarter!

I am clearly surprised by the news of the "toll" Chip paid with a quarter. Dominick is making sure he gets all of the conversation on his digital recorder.

We tried to figure out if the timing had been about the same, but I couldn't recall offhand at what point I started mentioning the toll and when I had asked Bob for the quarter. Fortunately, as Bob was videotaping our investigation, and the other group was also recording, the next day they were able to compare the quarter episodes. Chip sent me the following email:

"Just thought I'd let you know. While listening to the recorders, it was 16 mins in when you start to talk about the toll and it was also 16 mins in when Mark found that paper."

I think my jaw almost hit the keyboard when I read his message. Any slim chance that this had been a coincidence went out the window. In case this is all a little confusing, let me recap:

- We split up into two groups: our group went to the third floor, the other group went into the basement with no communication between the two groups.
- At 16 minutes into the investigation, Mark finds a piece of paper in the basement containing a joke that requires a quarter and gets Chip to give him a quarter.
- At the same exact time—16 minutes into the investigation—I start envisioning someone having to pay a quarter, and assume it has something to do with some sort of a toll at train station, or a nearby toll road. The image and message persist in my head until I finally ask Bob for a quarter, which I throw into one of the third floor rooms.
- Within minutes, I say that now that I have "paid the toll" I need a clear sign, and something knocks on the window sill directly behind me.
- The two groups don't meet for at least another hour, at which time we find out that we have each had an episode involving paying a quarter.

Where does this rate on the Paranormal Bizarro-Meter? On a scale of one to ten, this has to be a twenty-five...one for each of the twenty-five cents, that is.

And what do I think was going on here? Well, under other circumstances I might conclude that I had lost my marbles, but as this was all documented on video and audio I need to look for another explanation. My gut feel is that one of the restless spirits of the old train station wanted to give me an unmistakable validation of his presence, to let me know that whatever evidence we might obtain that night was not to be doubted. He is there, he is aware of what is going on, and he can prove it.

So when Mark found that paper and asked Chip for a quarter, this entity planted the thought in my head about paying a quarter, and didn't relent until I also asked Bob for a quarter. Once I had tossed the coin and asked for a clear sign, I was rewarded with the loud knocking right behind me.

Is this whole thing hard to believe? You bet it is! Even though it happened to me, I'm still having trouble digesting it. Do I have a better explanation? Absolutely not, as trying to assign this to pure coincidence would be even more ridiculous. On the whole cosmic scale of things, what are the chances that two isolated groups of people would have the same experience at the same time? My years of experience in the lab tell me that this is irrefutable proof of the existence of the paranormal—and the entire experiment only cost a couple of quarters!

I photographed the quarter on the floor where I had tossed it.

Actually, it only cost one quarter, because as soon as I heard Chip and Mark's story, I went back up to the third floor to photograph the quarter I tossed. Then I picked it up and brought it back to Bob. As of the time of the writing of this story, it is unknown as to whether Chip managed to get his quarter back from Mark, or if he is still an unwilling member of that club.

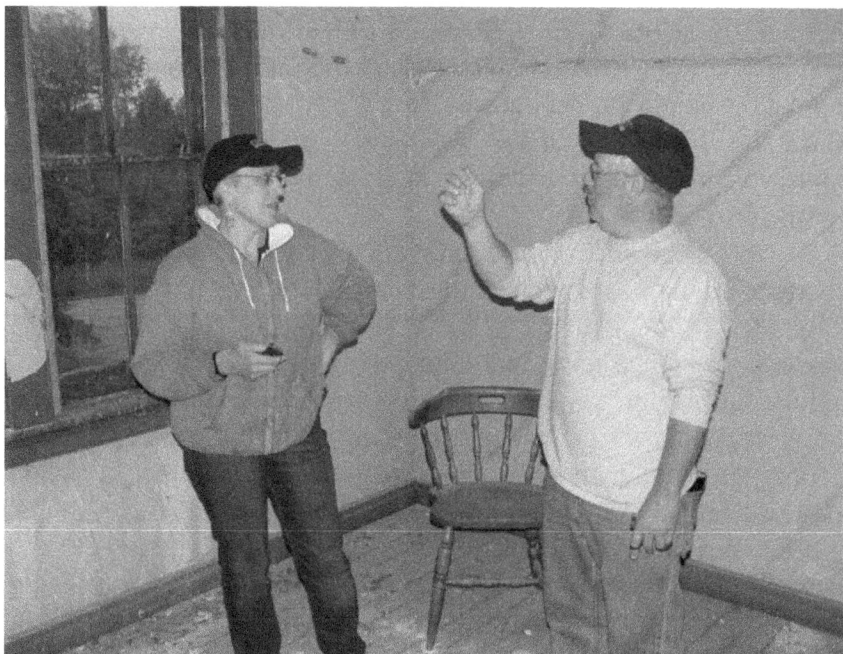

Chip describes some of the strange activity he has encountered.

That one episode would have made the entire night, but we still had the creepy basement to explore. As it was getting late for people who had to go to work early in the morning, it was just Bob, Mike, and I for the final leg of the investigation—and I got to carry the thermal camera! Let me tell you, I fell in love with that incredible piece of equipment—every girl should have one! You could actually trace someone's path by the residual heat of their footprints; how cool is that?

One thing I did learn about the shortcomings of the device is that you have to be very careful about reflections giving you false images. It seems that body heat reflects off of all kinds of surfaces so you have to be completely aware of who is where at all times. If you think you see a human form, make everyone present move back and forth to see if the image is simply a reflection of a real human being. Just using the thermal imager for a few minutes made me very suspicious of some of the alleged "evidence" I have seen by ghost hunting groups on TV.

Unfortunately, the only thing I detected in the darkness of the basement was a lone mouse making a mad dash between piles of trash on the floor. If owls and cats had thermal imagers, the rodent population would be decimated! And I pity the poor criminal who thinks he can hide under the cover of darkness when law enforcement has this technology at its disposal. (Actually, I don't pity the criminals at all!)

Even though nothing unusual was visible in the basement, Bob reported that he heard whispering behind him. All three of us later heard what I thought sounded like a squealing sound, and suspected someone's stomach to be the culprit. However, both Mike and Bob said the noise hadn't come from them, and they both felt it sounded like a woman's voice. As they were closer to the source, I had to defer to their judgment. My digital recorder did pick up the sound, but it was faint and I couldn't make anything out of it.

We next checked out the first floor, but nothing further occurred. It was getting late and had started to rain, so we decided to forego any outdoor investigating and pack it up for the night.

So, what can I conclude from our latest train station adventure? It is one very haunted location, with most likely more than one spirit roaming around. I would like to be able to find some records of the station masters who lived there, as I hope to find someone named Simon. I feel that the dark shadow I saw and the wheezing breaths were from someone who may have died in the building of some type of disease of the lungs. I also think Herbie is still in residence, along with at least one elusive and mischievous child. And then there is the remarkable quarter episode, which unquestionably has become one of the top experiences in my almost 15 years of ghost hunting.

The property is currently for sale, and hopefully, this historic old train station won't meet with the wrecking ball. While the land is overgrown and the structure stands empty, there is still a silent dignity to the place. With some hard work, a substantial budget, and a couple of new staircases, it could be restored into a wonderful restaurant or bed & breakfast.

If the place does reopen some day, staff and guests should be forewarned: The old expression "a penny for your thoughts" doesn't apply here. They will cost you at least a quarter...

On both sides of the thermal camera:
Me using the camera, and a thermal image of me.

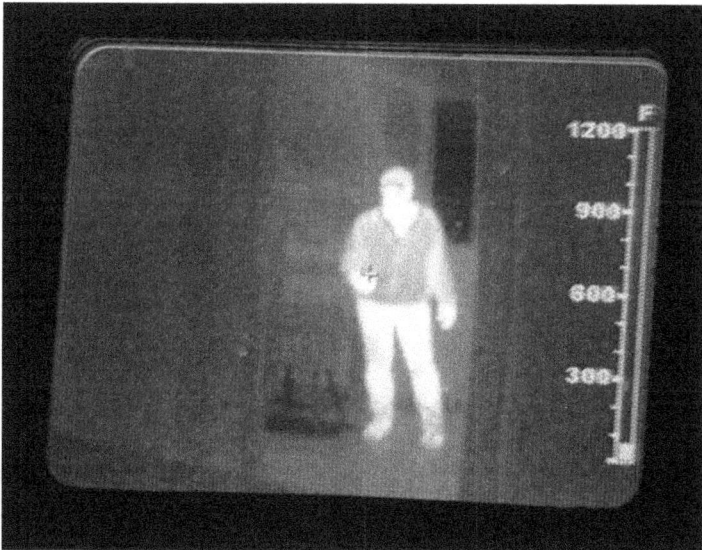

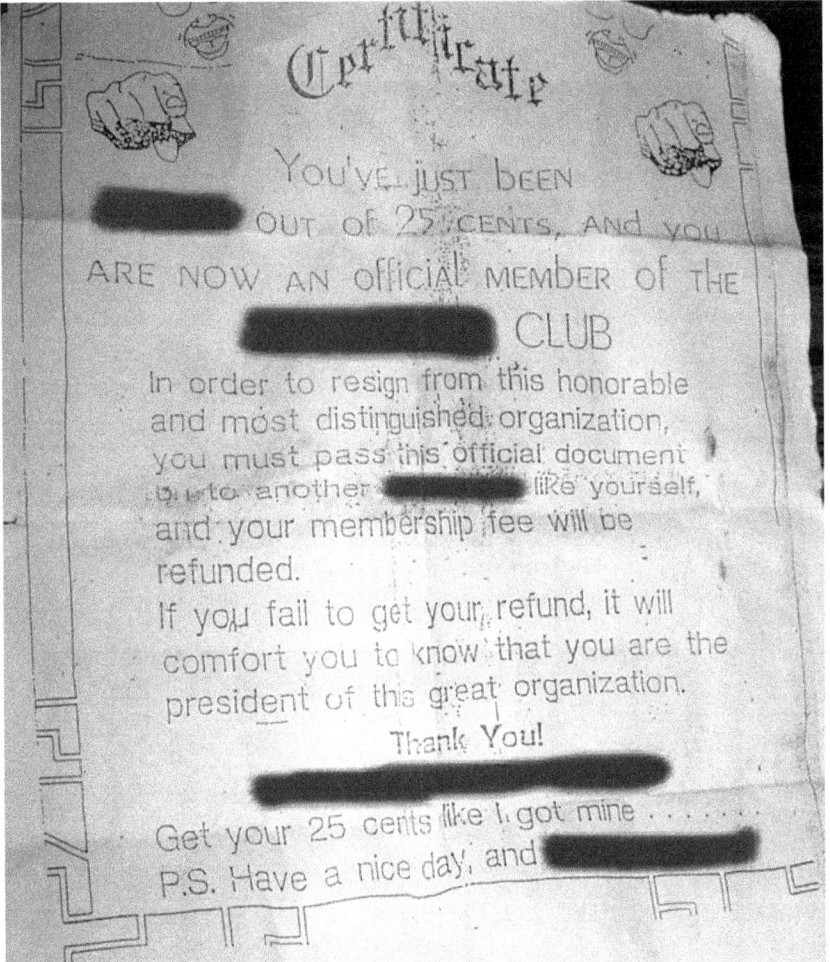

Certificate

You've just been ███████ out of 25 cents, and you are now an official member of the ███████ CLUB

In order to resign from this honorable and most distinguished organization, you must pass this official document on to another ███████ like yourself, and your membership fee will be refunded.

If you fail to get your refund, it will comfort you to know that you are the president of this great organization.

Thank You!

███████████████████

Get your 25 cents like I got mine . . . .

P.S. Have a nice day, and ███████

I had to censor the certificate that
was found which asks for a 25 cents.

124

Greenfield Park Museum
Greenfield Park, New York

The Quaker Meeting House

There are coincidences in life, and then there are some sneaky orchestrations by forces we can't fathom that sometimes bring everything together. On a Wednesday morning in June of 2009, psychic Lisa Ann was talking to a friend of hers, who is also a psychic. The friend asked where her upcoming ghost hunt was taking place, and Lisa Ann replied that she had no plans. In fact, she had actually just canceled one that would have taken place in a few days. Undaunted, the friend insisted she would be going on a ghost hunt very soon, and Lisa Ann equally insisted she wasn't.

That afternoon, Lisa Ann was in Port Jervis working on a missing person case and she called Mike Worden—a detective with the Port Jervis police—to ask a few questions. Mike mentioned that

125

he and I were having dinner, and asked if she would care to join us. And by the way—would she also be interested in joining us on a ghost investigation that evening?

The investigation of the Greenfield Park Museum had been in the works for some time, and had actually been postponed from the previous week, so it was nice when all the little pieces came together on what was apparently the right time on the right day. As per our standard operating procedures of not divulging any details of a location to Lisa Ann, during dinner we did not discuss the one-room schoolhouse, Quaker meeting house, and cemetery that comprise the museum—but even if I had wanted to I couldn't, as I didn't know any of the details, either. Barbara Bleitzhofer had arranged the investigation with local historian Al Perry, and she had not told me what they had found on previous visits. So we were all flying equally blind, which as it turned out, helped in a very key piece of validation.

As soon as we arrived, without even getting out of the car, Lisa Ann saw "a little, old man" in front of the cemetery who she felt used to be a caretaker. His wife had died and he was lonely in his later years, and caring for the property gave him purpose in life. His name was Sam or Samuel, and he was apparently very curious as to what we were doing there!

Fast forward about twenty minutes later when Barbara, Al, and his wife, Gwen, arrived. While Lisa Ann was exploring the back part of the cemetery, I mentioned to Barbara about the man named Sam—and she almost tackled me in excitement! In her other visits, Barbara had numerous "conversations" with the spirit of an old man named Sam, who she also believed used to take care of the place. And, they had already found a Samuel in the records who did indeed look after the property.

Well that didn't take long! Often, months or years of research may be necessary to sense a specific name and then find that name in records. Here, in just a few minutes, we had Lisa Ann meet Sam, Barbara reveal that she had already met the same spirit, and his identity was already confirmed in the records. As Mike put it, if we had gotten back in the car and left right then and there, it still would have been a great investigation!

Speaking of Mike, the night must have been a bit unusual for him, as the first graves we saw bore the name Worden. In fact, half the cemetery seemed to be Wordens, or as I believe I have said on another occasion, "There were more Wordens than people!" It is possible that they were ancestors, so it will be interesting to see what some genealogical research reveals. In any event, it couldn't have been the most comforting thing to see your name on tombstones everywhere you looked.

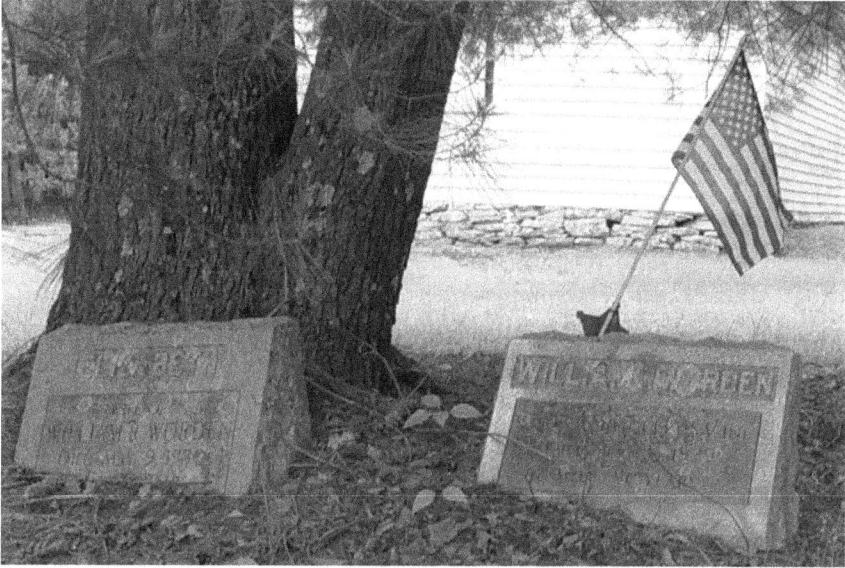

Two of the many Worden gravestones.

The Quaker Meeting House was built in 1818, and is about as plain and unadorned as you can get—but then the Quakers wouldn't have it any other way. The single room inside the building was divided down the middle with a partial wall so as to separate the men from the women, and the benches couldn't have been more uncomfortable. As comfortable seating + long-winded sermons = rapidly falling asleep, it is doubtful that any church seating has ever been designed with comfort in mind.

The men sat on the left side and the women on the right, and Barbara told me that on previous investigations they had sensed that a spirit would get annoyed if they didn't follow protocol and stay on their proper sides. Naturally, I planted myself on the men's side to see if I could get a reaction, and Mike—who had not heard what Barbara had told me—said that he sensed that some irritated presence was saying, "What is *she* doing there?"

Boards could be placed along the center partition to complete the wall between the male and female sections. The hard, narrow benches are remarkably uncomfortable.

Lisa Ann had expected this building to exude peace and quiet, so she was quite shocked when she stepped inside and felt anguish, disease, and death. The picture that emerged was of a time between 1850-53, when some sort of epidemic hit the community, with the children being particularly vulnerable. She felt the panic and anxiety of the parents who tried to save the sick children that were lined up on the right side of the room. Stepping over into the left side, she experienced a deep sense of sadness and mourning, as this is where the bodies of the children who expired had been placed.

Later in the cemetery, Lisa Ann found an area where she believed the children's bodies had been cremated. She also said that we wouldn't find any carved gravestones with the names of these children, because only a few plain rocks had been placed at the site.

128

Barbara and Lisa Ann on the female side of the building,
discussing the terrible epidemic that may have left
an indelible impression in this building.

The next day I did some research, as my knowledge of the Quakers
was limited, and I found that cremation was an acceptable practice
for them. I was also surprised to find that prior to 1852, carved
gravestones *were prohibited*, so had these children died in 1850-51,
they would not have their names and dates of death placed on
stones!

I also found that between 1850-53, New York was hit by
epidemics of yellow fever, cholera, and influenza. Whether any of
these epidemics hit Ulster County, though, or more specifically the
Quaker population, will require further research.

Next we walked across the street to the one-room schoolhouse,
which was built in the early 1800s. Remarkably, the school was still
in use until the late 1950s! The building is flanked by "his and her"
outhouses and a wood shed. I definitely recommend visiting this
schoolhouse, as you truly step back through time when you enter the
single room with its rows of old-fashioned desks. A woodstove in
the center of the room was the sole source of heat in the long, cold

winters. The teacher sat up on a platform—the better to keep an eye on unruly or dishonest children!

The schoolhouse, flanked by the his and her outhouses
and the wood shed.

Apart from the ever-present Sam in the schoolhouse, there didn't seem to be any other active spirits. There were residual impressions, and Lisa Ann did get the names of several former students, including Robert, Sarah, and Harold. All in all, the old school room was a peaceful place, where nothing of great note happened that night.

Professor Mike bringing the class to order.

The wood shed was another story, and it was a very bad story.

Barbara opened the door to the shed and stepped aside to allow Lisa Ann to enter. I noticed that Barbara did not follow her in so I assumed there was something unpleasant about the place, but even so, I was not prepared for what hit me. I took one step into the small building, my hair stood on end, I felt awful, and immediately heard the word, "rape." I took one picture of Lisa Ann and walked right back out.

"I know what I'm sensing, but I won't say anything until Lisa Ann is finished," I said walking over to Mike, and then whispered to him, "It's rape."

Just moments later, Lisa Ann emerged from the wood shed and said that she felt young girls had been raped and molested in that shed. Upon hearing that, Barbara declared that was exactly what she had sensed on previous visits, and Gwen confirmed that was what Barbara had told her many times before. It was a terrible thing considering the circumstances, but quite remarkable nonetheless that three women independently had the exact same reaction in this seemingly innocuous old wood shed.

Mike then went inside and also did not stay long. Though he felt very uncomfortable in there, he did not have the same sense of violation as we did, so it may be something that presents itself most clearly to women, for obvious reasons. Lisa Ann felt that the violator may have been the son of the Headmaster of the school, so the unfortunate victims were afraid to speak out against him.

This was a prime example of how you never know what to expect on a ghost investigation, and how these awful crimes leave an indelible imprint on the scene for many, many years. This unpleasant episode is also an excellent illustration of the fact that haunted places are not amusement parks, and if you have such an attitude, you have no place being at a site such as this. Of course, humor has its function to occasionally break the tension, but you need to be respectful of what people suffered.

The revelations of the wood shed certainly put a damper on the mood of the group, but we did need to continue and spend more time at each site. Unfortunately, it started raining, so we decided to skip any further investigation in the cemetery—more for the sake of our equipment than ourselves. Lisa Ann had to leave as she was co-hosting her radio show later that night, so the five of us went back to the Quaker Meeting House for some quiet time, as well as some Q & A.

Mike sat in the back corner of the men's side for a while, and began to get a skin-crawling sensation. I checked out the area around him and did find a few wispy cobwebs, so the mystery was solved. But the episode did lead to the funniest line of the night.

Barbara at the door to the dreaded wood shed.

When Gwen confirmed that she also saw the fine filaments, Al replied, "I'm surprised you're able to see cobwebs here. You never seem to see them at home!"

Our attempt at some quiet time failed miserably, as there were noisy children playing in some nearby yards, someone was mowing their lawn, and it seemed as though we must have been in the direct flight path for a major airport. The schoolhouse was a bit quieter, but nothing turned up on our recorders. Still, it was a remarkably successful investigation, and a great example of how you don't always have to stay until the wee hours of the morning to get great results.

I am hoping some research will uncover pertinent facts about the epidemic that may have claimed so many young lives. I would also be curious to see if any photos of Sam surface. But haunted or not, the quaint one-room schoolhouse and Quaker Meeting House offer a rare glimpse into a much simpler time that was not all that long ago. And if you do want to sample the paranormal side of the Greenfield Park Museum, keep a sharp lookout for Sam, because he will be sure to be keeping an eye on you!

For more information and visiting hours:

Greenfield Park Museum
Rte 52 W
Greenfield Park, NY 12435
Phone: (845) 647-6560

Mike in the cobweb corner of the Quaker Meeting House.

Lisa Ann communicating with Sam.

Lisa Ann in the wood shed.

Lisa Ann can be contacted through her website at:

www.spiritquesthealingcenter.com

Boulderberg Manor Revisited
Tomkins Cove, New York

All photos in this story courtesy of Michael Worden

One of the places I am most frequently asked about is Boulderberg Manor in Tomkins Cove, New York. It was a popular restaurant in the 1970s, and a generation of local residents has very fond memories of spending first dates and special occasions there. They also have many memories of encountering ghosts.

The house was built in 1858 by Calvin Tomkins, who lived to the ripe old age of 99. The man who owned the place during the Depression did not enjoy such a long lifespan, but then that was due to the fact that he committed suicide. His bank had failed, and in despair he took his own life in one of the third floor bedrooms. There are other stories of murders and other deaths here, but it's often difficult to separate fact from fiction.

There is one fact of which I can be certain: I visited the old manor house in 1998 and the stories the owner related convinced me that this place is indeed very haunted. I wrote about the visit in my very first ghost book, *Ghosts of Rockland County*, (which can also now be found in *Ghost Investigator, Volume 1*), but at the time this was all very new to me and I didn't have the opportunity, equipment or experience to conduct a full investigation. For the past eleven years, I have been hoping to get back to Boulderberg for a more in-depth look. That chance finally arrived in July of 2009.

I was very excited about returning and told Mike he absolutely had to come as it was such an amazing place. While there were a couple of sections of the house that gave me the creeps in 1998, overall it was a place of light and beauty, and the owners and their many dogs seemed quite contented. I was not prepared for how different the house feels now.

I think my initial reaction was, "Could this be the same place?"

It looked the same as I remembered, but there is now an oppressive sadness and darkness permeating the property. Mike immediately felt ill at ease, and, in fact, never felt comfortable the entire night. What had happened to this house? Why had it shifted toward the negative?

Our suspicions of increased activity, tending toward the negative, were confirmed when we spoke to the owners Linda and Barbara, Barbara's daughter Vanessa, their friend Debbie, and her daughter Alanna. The following is just some of the activity that has occurred in the two years they have owned the old house.

When they first went to look at the property, they saw a man in a tan suit, looking very formal and proper, and assumed he was there to show the place. When speaking to the realtor later, they discovered that no such man existed, and no one was living in the house at the time.

Vanessa, who has been experiencing things since childhood, felt a presence as soon as she entered the house. She lived there alone for about six months and the first direct encounter came in a third floor bedroom, where she saw a distinct silhouette of a man. Just about every night there were doors opening and closing, knocking, strange sounds, and apparitions that appeared in her room. On several occasions she even heard her name being called.

Barbara, Linda, and Debbie share their stories while
I take notes. There are beautiful views of the Hudson River from
this terrace and throughout the property.

During this period of time, a skeptical friend volunteered to house-sit and take care of the pets while Vanessa was away. He didn't believe in ghosts, but his attitude toward the supernatural changed radically. One night when he was upstairs he heard a very loud argument downstairs between two women, and assumed the owners had come in. Not wanting to stick his nose into the heated dispute, he stayed upstairs, until he heard something else. Someone had started playing a grand piano, but there wasn't a piano in the house! He ran downstairs and searched every room, but couldn't find anyone or any source of the music.

Both Vanessa and Barbara have been pushed, and objects have been thrown across the room. Shadows and images of someone hanging have also been seen. Strange reflections appear in mirrors. Barbara will make a bed and a few minutes later the covers would all be rumpled, which is something that also happened to previous owners.

Vanessa relates her experiences from her time alone in the house.

Barbara also sees many apparitions, including a woman in an old fashioned long, red dress. The woman's hair is pulled back and she may have been a servant as she appears to be cleaning and trying to look after the property. Visitors have also seen this woman, along with many other inexplicable images. One friend actually refused to even pass through the gate to the house because she felt so uncomfortable.

The pets also act strangely, which is exactly what happened when I first visited eleven years earlier. The owner at that time had many dogs, and they happily followed wherever she went—until she got to the third floor. Then they became very agitated, their hair stood up, they growled and whined, and none of them would enter the bedroom where the man committed suicide. Similarly today, the dogs and cats watch things that others can't see, act nervous for no apparent reason, growl and bark in certain parts of the house, and generally act in inexplicable ways—unless we accept the fact that they have sixth senses we don't understand.

After a tour of the house and listening to everyone's experiences, Alanna, Mike, and I sat quietly in the "China Room," so called because of the red Oriental wallpaper. The woman who had invited me in 1998 had died in this room several years later after a long illness, and I couldn't help but think of her. However, Mike and Alanna, who is also sensitive to spirits and energies, kept picturing a man. They both described him as having dark hair, and being dressed in clothing from the early decades of the twentieth century.

The most prevalent feature of this man was the overwhelming sense of sadness, anxiety, and depression. Mike pictured him pacing back and forth, contemplating suicide. Alanna also saw him as someone who struggled with the decision to end his life. We assumed it was the banker who killed himself in the 1930s, but we can't rule out that there may have been another suicide in that house over the past 150 years.

Alanna senses a presence in the suicide room.

We also sat quietly on the third floor. We did hear some tapping and a faint metallic sound, but not knowing the natural sounds of the house—and knowing other people were in the house at the time—we couldn't say for certain where the sounds were coming from. We also couldn't place the source of a very bad odor, one best described as something rotting. Alanna first caught the scent of it in the suicide room. Mike smelled it, too, so we assumed that it was a mouse or squirrel that may have died in the wall. However, the unpleasant smell seemed to follow wherever we went, and it did not persist in any one spot. The odor came and went as if it had a mind of its own, and perhaps it did.

Unfortunately, our time was limited that night, and there was simply too much space to cover—over 8,500 square feet!—so we will have to return and spend the entire night to try to get the full experience.

Boulderberg Manor is a place that needs some thorough investigating, both of the paranormal activity, as well as the history of the people who lived there. What secrets are hidden between its thick, fortress-like walls? Why have the spirits of the house become so restless? Let's hope I don't have to wait another 11 years to find out.

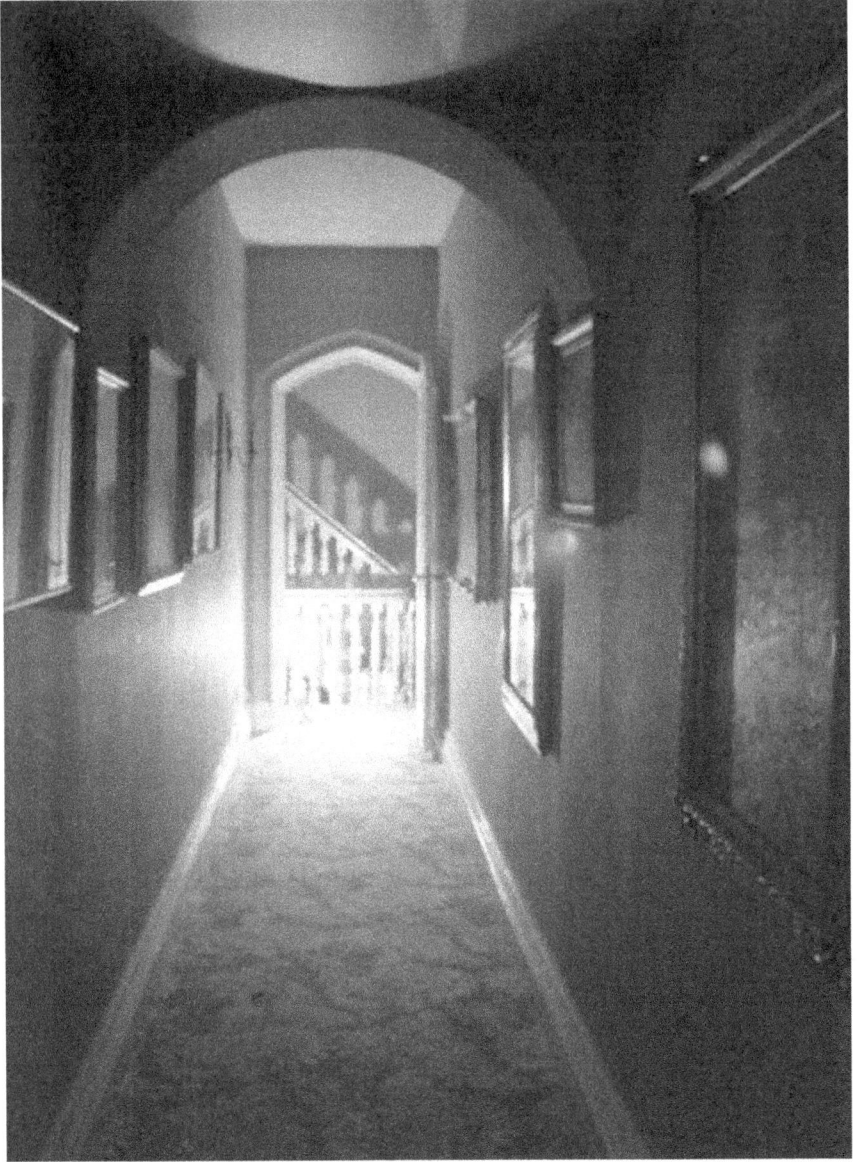

The hallway between the stairs and the China Room. (Infrared image.)
This is a very active section of the house.

Mike is on full alert on the main staircase
between the second and third floor.
(Infrared image.)

What secrets are within the walls of this old manor house?

Stalking from the Grave
Westchester County, NY

When I was out of commission, Mike Worden was a life saver stepping in to help. Among other things, he was a terrific speaker when presenting lectures from *Ghost Investigator Volume 8*, and he did a great job on a couple of investigations I was unable to attend.

This is a case in Westchester County, New York, where a cop and his fiancée were being tormented in their apartment. They couldn't stand living there anymore so were moving out, and Mike got a chance to investigate the week they were leaving. The following will be presented as excerpts from Mike's report on the case. It is clear from his observations that his years of police work served him well!

***

The building is a small apartment house that looks like it was a single family home at one point that was sectioned off into multiple units. "Ed" lived in the apartment for about three years and was in the process of moving out, and would be moving into another place with his fiancée, "Nancy."

Ed wrote this about his experiences:

"I moved into the apartment a few years ago and immediately began to see 'something.' My fiancée has been scratched, and there has been writing on the mirror. I am moving out and there isn't much left in the apartment but even as I was there today I saw movement in the hallway. I have had TV's fall from sturdy platforms and the sound of the toilet bowl closing although I know the seat is down."

He told me that he had noticed activity after about two months of living in the apartment. He would see something passing in the hallway while he was in the living room. He described it as feeling "as when you turn around you would think you see something but there is nothing there."

The downstairs neighbor told Ed that she has never noticed anything out of the ordinary.

During the interview with Nancy, she described a lifetime of experiences with the paranormal and related to me that she felt the entity in Ed's apartment was attached to her and following her.

She explained that as a young teenager she was victimized by an older boy in the neighborhood and that no one believed her. She stated that this person ended up dying several years ago of cancer, but had been a habitual drug user and she suspected AIDS. She reported seeing him shortly before he died at a picnic and wishing the worst death upon him.

During the investigation there was little to no EMF activity. In the bedroom, where a TV had fallen inexplicably, there were a few spikes but nothing out of the ordinary.

I had set up motion detectors and the K-II meter and Tri Field in this room and had Ed and Nancy in the room as we began to summon whatever was in the house. We were calling this person by name, call him "George," and at first nothing was happening. Ed and I began to challenge the spirit a bit by telling him that he could not be near Nancy and that he was not welcome here or anywhere around her.

The atmosphere changed and became heavy. I smelled a mixture of body odor and alcohol in the air. Nancy said that she felt this man in the room and said she smelled him. I asked her to clarify, and told her that I smelled something, but not what it was, and she said that the night she was victimized, he smelled of booze and body odor.

A couple of times during this Nancy complained of being touched. During this time there was a definite male energy in the room and it was a negative energy. It seemed to grow in intensity by being provoked. This is a case where provocation was appropriate: the spirit was thought to be that of a male specifically targeting Nancy.

The original provocation was ineffective as we were trying to call the spirit a coward and telling him that he deserved what he got and he was afraid to come into the room because we [Ed and I] were there. We then took a different approach which was to directly tell him he was to leave her alone, to stay away from her, that he was not welcomed there or anywhere she was and that he had to move on. This is when there was a shift.

146

The Tri Field and K-II never alarmed. Nothing was on video or audio. The motion alarms never activated.

Eventually the atmosphere shifted after Ed and I repeatedly told the spirit, assuming it was this George, to move on and to leave her alone and to go on to what is waiting for him. The negative male presence seemed to leave and the atmosphere in the room became comfortable and I did not smell that mixture of BO and alcohol.

I note that Nancy did not mention that odor to me PRIOR to the experience and that the odor was simultaneous to the sudden negative male presence in the room. This is about the time Nancy complained of being touched and feeling that this person was there and she was also smelling the odor.

***

Was this negative male entity trying to victimize Nancy again from beyond the grave? Ed photographed the following scratches that suddenly appeared on Nancy's back, although the black and white picture does not do justice to the red, swollen lines.

On another occasion, they found the words "I" and "HER" written on the bathroom mirror. A message from the dead stalker?

Ed's identity was obscured to protect his privacy.

As I have always said, death does not improve one's personality, and if George had derived some sick pleasure victimizing Nancy in life, could he still be attempting to satisfy his twisted desires from beyond the grave? Or was it some other dark entity in that apartment, preying upon the innocent? Whatever the case, Ed and Nancy hope they never cross paths with him again...

One final note: I am very pleased to announce that Mike Worden is working on his first book, which will highlight his many years of experience with the paranormal. For more information please visit his website at:

www.paranormalpolice.com

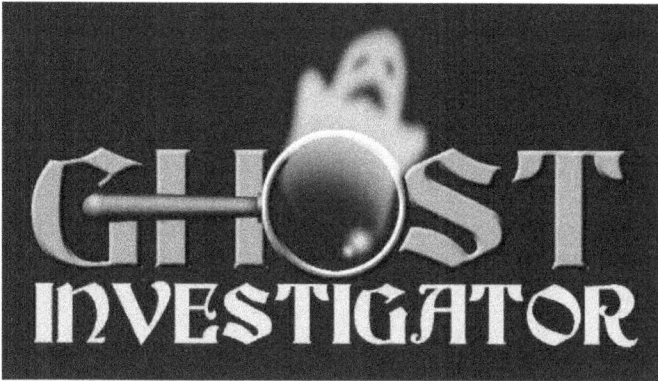

To order books, get info, and share your haunting,
contact the Ghost Investigator through:

www.ghostinvestigator.com

Or write to:

Linda Zimmermann
P.O. Box 192
Blooming Grove, NY 10914

Or send email to:

linda@gotozim.com

Copy this page to use for your own ghost hunt. If you know of a haunted site you think should be considered for an upcoming book, please contact me at:

P.O. Box 192, Blooming Grove, NY, 10914

www.ghostinvestigator.com

Field Report

Date: **Location:**

Time In: **Weather:**

Names of People Interviewed:

Equipment: Camera ☐ **Video** ☐ **Audio Recorder**
☐ **Thermometer** **Other:**

Experiences: **Sounds** ☐ **Odors** ☐ **Cold Spots** ☐

Visuals ☐ **Touch/Sensations** ☐ **Movement** ☐

Details (Attach extra sheet if necessary):

Time Out: **Total Time on Site:**

Conclusions:

Prepared and Signed by:

Witness(es):

Other books by Linda Zimmermann

Dead Center
A Ghost Hunter Novel

When one of the country's largest shopping centers is built in Virginia, rumors abound that the place is haunted by ghosts of Civil War soldiers. Ghost hunter Sarah Brooks must uncover the truth, and come face to face with the restless spirits that walk through the *Dead Center*.

Okay, Sarah Brooks. This is what you do, she said to herself. *This is who you are.*

Closing her eyes, Sarah spun around and counted to three. When she opened her eyes, she had to clamp her hand over her mouth to stifle a scream. There was a pale, misty shape of a man drawing closer. It was like an image being projected into a fog, and it rippled, wavered, then slowly began to take on a more defined shape. The wounded man behind her screamed as if Death himself was coming to take him...

Ghost Investigator Volume 1: *Hauntings of the Hudson Valley*
Ghost Investigator Volume 2: *From Gettysburg to Lizzie Borden*
Ghost Investigator Volume 3
Ghost Investigator Volume 4: *Ghosts of New York and New Jersey*
Ghost Investigator Volume 5: *From Beyond the Grave*
Ghost Investigator Volume 6: *Dark Shadows*
Ghost Investigator Volume 7: *Psychic Impressions*
Ghost Investigator Volume 8: *Back Into the Light*

www.ingramcontent.com/pod-product-compliance
Lightning Source LLC
LaVergne TN
LVHW011237080426
835509LV00005B/532